D0091559

10
Days
to Faster Reading

Also by The Princeton Language Institute

Grammar 101
Guide to Pronunciation
Roget's 21st Century Thesaurus

Also by Abby Marks Beale

Success Skills: Strategies for Lifelong Learning

10 Days to Faster Reading

The Princeton Language Institute
and Abby Marks Beale

Produced by The Philip Lief Group, Inc.

GRAND CENTRAL
PUBLISHING

NEW YORK   BOSTON

Produced by The Philip Lief Group, Inc.

Grand Central Publishing
Hachette Book Group USA
237 Park Avenue
New York, NY 10017

Visit our Web site at www.HachetteBookGroupUSA.com

Printed in the United States of America

First Printing: July 2001

10   9

Grand Central Publishing is a division of Hachette Book Group USA, Inc.
The Grand Central Publishing name and logo is a trademark of Hachette Book Group USA, Inc.

Library of Congress Cataloging-in-Publication Data
Marks Beal, Abby.
    10 days to faster reading / [edited by] the Princeton Language Institute ; Abby Marks Beale.
        p.   cm.
    ISBN 978-0-446-67667-0
    1. Speed reading.   I. Title: Ten days to faster reading.   II. Princeton Language Institute.   III. Title.
LB1050.54.M37 2001
428.4'32—dc21   00-053413

Book design by Ralph Fowler
Cover design by Jon Valk
Icon illustrations by Max Crandall

For Christopher

Acknowledgments

This book is a reality because of the help and support of the following individuals:

My husband, Chris, who tolerated my early morning absences and reviewed each chapter before submission.

My kids, who provided me with the humor breaks I desperately needed.

My mother, for instilling an early love of reading, which I forgot about until I was way past my college years.

Christopher Lee, who provided me with the incredibly powerful car racing analogies and jargon.

Pamela Mullan, who provided insight about speed reading in her essay "The History of Speed Reading," included in Days 4 and 5, and her many valuable contributions too numerous to mention.

Louise Loomis, director of the Critical Thinking Center for Creativity and Problem-Solving (Hartford, Connecticut), for her contribution to Day 6 on the "Nine Guidelines for Critical Reading."

John Whitman, whose writing talent is displayed in many of the timed reading activities.

Jamie Saxon and Eileen Koutnik, my editors at The Philip Lief Group, who answered my questions and kept me on schedule.

Other authors and researchers in the field of reading too numerous to mention, whose wisdom and insights I have learned and subsequently shared.

The participants in my workshops, who ask great questions and prove to me time and again why I do this for a living.

Contents

Day 8

Day 9

Day 10

Introduction

Congratulations! By having this book in your hands, you have taken a very important step in improving your reading skills. Since you probably have not had any reading training since elementary school, now you will learn something new about how to read more efficiently and effectively.

You may be a busy professional looking to get through your reading workload or master new material more quickly, an interested educator looking for strategies for your students, a homemaker or retiree looking to develop your reading skills, or a student who'd like to know the magic involved in faster reading. Whatever the reason, you've chosen the right book. By reading this book and using the information daily, you *will* learn all you need to know about how to read faster and improve your comprehension.

But what does "reading this book" mean? Each chapter builds on the previous one. I encourage you to read the chapters in the order in which they are presented to maximize your speed reading potential. The book has these key objectives:

- **Help you realize the value of what you may already be doing.** Throughout this book, you will find many concepts that you are already familiar with yet you may not have known that they were good reading strategies. You will be able to identify several positive things that you are already doing that no one formally taught you, but rather, due to survival or ingenuity, you have figured out on your own.

- **Introduce you to a wide spectrum of ideas to pick and choose from.** There is no one best way to read. But there are many great strategies you can use. This book is not intended as a book of rules but rather a book of options. This is why you are asked to try the strategies, think about the concepts, and eventually decide which will work best for you. The last pages of this book are blank. Use them to write down your "keepers"—the most important or valuable ideas you personally got from this book. Doing so keeps you actively looking for what you want and documents your keepers for later review.

- **Enhance your level of reading confidence.** For many people, reading is something they do, not something they love. Many readers think they are the slowest readers in the world or feel inadequate in their overall reading abilities. True or not, one thing is certain: If you do not feel confident in your reading ability or do not get satisfaction when you read, then you won't choose to read. When you reach a point where you feel like the time you spend reading is worthwhile, because you understand or get what you need from it, then you will choose to read more often. It is that simple.

I also recommend you keep the following materials handy to help you do the exercises in each chapter:

- Pencil or pen
- Highlighter
- Paper
- Calculator

- Watch with a second hand or stopwatch
- Blank 3 x 5 white index card or the blank side of a business card
- Familiar reading material such as favorite magazines or newspapers

You are a reader who wants to learn how to become skilled at speed reading. A comparable relationship exists between car drivers and those who want to learn how to become skilled at race car driving. Therefore, I have used a race car theme, drawing analogies between speed reading and car racing. You do not have to be a race car fan, of course, to appreciate the connection.

Practice is an important aspect of improving your reading speed. Each day has a practice reading called a Time Trial. Most contain four hundred words, very short in comparison to newspaper or magazine articles, and are followed by a series of ten comprehension statements to answer. You will be able to track your progress in your Words per Minute on page 207, which you will add to your Personal Progress chart on pages 203 to 206.

The comprehension statements ask you to choose among three possible answers: True (T), False (F), or Not Discussed (N). All your answers need to come from the information in the reading, not from what you may already know.

Though this book will show you how to efficiently read anything, most of the information is focused on reading nonfiction such as business books and periodicals or school textbooks. Nonfiction readers are always looking for ways to read more in less time. Fiction readers, who enjoy reading stories and novels, have a choice. As a result, you will find that all the Time Trials in this book are nonfiction except for one fiction reading on Day 7.

If, after finishing this book, you have lingering questions or concerns or want to share your success with me, please write to me:

Abby Marks Beale
The Corporate Educator
P.O. Box 4212
Wallingford, CT 06492
www.RevItUpReading.com
www.TheCorporateEducator.com

Enough said. Have fun at the races!

10
Days

to Faster Reading

Putting the Key
in the Ignition

Think of this book as a key that enables you to jump-start your reading abilities and test-drive a whole new set of skills and techniques. If you are like many, you already feel confident about having this book in your hand because learning to read faster is a goal you have set many times. Now, by opening this book, you are closer than ever to achieving that goal.

How Will Increasing My Reading Speed Help Me?

As you sit poised in the driver's seat, let's look at the benefits of becoming a faster reader:

- **Read more in less time.** You will double or even triple the amount you read in the same amount of time. At times, you may find that you only have to skim material.

- **Improve your concentration.** The faster you read, the more you pay attention and focus on what you are doing.

- **Understand material with greater depth and accuracy.** As your concentration improves, you will better understand what you read.

- **Retain information better.** You can remember information better because you are paying attention, concentrating, and understanding more.

- **Enjoy reading more.** The faster reading strategies in this book help you build confidence and competence in your reading abilities, so you quickly find you enjoy reading more.

Following are some more little known benefits of learning to read faster—benefits I have personally experienced or participants in my workshops have shared with me. (I know there are more than these and maybe someday you'll let me know what they are.)

- Receive higher test scores if you are continuing your education, such as going to law or graduate school.

- Feel more in control of information overload.

- Surf the Web more efficiently.

- Skim directions on how to assemble, plug in, and/or operate any apparatus, toy, or child plaything you need in a hurry.

- Scan and compare nutrition labels with greater ease (cut your shopping time).

- Know how long reading really takes and plan accordingly.

For me, using faster reading skills has greatly benefited my professional life. But the most powerful example I can relate is one from my personal life. When my first child was about nine months old, he woke up in the middle of the night crying with a barking cough that sounded like a seal. Now, as an experienced parent, I know that this is a medical condition called croup, which constricts the airway, making breathing difficult. Inexperienced as I was then, I was terrified. I called the pediatrician's answering service and left an urgent message. While waiting for the return call, I searched through my parenting books to figure out what was wrong and how I could make it better. Within minutes, by scanning the indexes, skimming the text, and applying the advice, my son was on his way to better breathing—and my own breathing began to return to normal as well. This scenario has played itself out time and again. Each time I am acutely aware of how helpful faster reading skills are.

Work with a Pro at Your Side

To really make a difference in your reading abilities, you must experiment with and apply the ideas in this book. Imagine that you are new to car racing and are being groomed to become a race car driver, a faster reader. Though you may already know how to drive a car, already know how to read, driving a race car is a completely different experience. If you were told to get behind the wheel of a race car and enter a competition right now, your current driving skills and knowledge base would be inadequate. However, imagine you were given ten days to prepare for the race. In those ten days you worked with a pro (this book), and discovered through trial and error techniques, tips, and trade secrets from the pros—in short, you'd find what works best for you.

So, put yourself in the driver's seat. Remember, although you will find some great ideas in this book, they will remain just great ideas if you do not turn on the ignition and explore the roadways of faster reading.

Five Reasons to Get in the Race

There are five reasons you might be stuck in neutral with your reading ability:

Your Attitude

Mentally, quickly fill in the blank of the following statement with the word or words that best describes you:

I am a(n) _____ reader.

When I begin a workshop with this statement, I solicit responses from the audience. Immediately, some participants call out "slow," "lazy," and "non-." Others say "avid" or "voracious." Still others describe their reading level as "poky," "buried," or "sleepy." I know with a more positive response, such as avid or voracious, you are someone who chooses to read more and spend more time reading than if you use a more negative term to describe your reading.

If you believe you fit into the category of slow or lazy, I venture to guess that reading is not a very satisfying experience for you. You may daydream a lot or believe you read at a snail's pace. You may find yourself rereading sentences or paragraphs frequently because you didn't get it the first time, or even after rereading you still didn't get it. You get bored easily and don't understand why people read for pleasure.

Are you wondering how I might know you so well? Well, I am describing how I used to feel and act as a reader before I learned the secrets to being a good one. I wasn't always the efficient, active reader I am now. I also believe that the more successful people in the world read widely and are voracious readers. Being successful doesn't necessarily mean making a lot of money. It does mean being competent at what you do. Learning and growing through reading helps you to become professionally and personally successful. If you ask anyone who is prominent in their field to discuss how they got to where they are right now, I can almost guarantee you that their path to success included a lot of reading.

Even if you filled in the blank with a word like avid or voracious, you may want to increase your reading load at home or work but are not sure the best way to achieve that goal. Or, you are looking for a reason to pat yourself on the back for a job well done.

Throughout this book, I will ask you again to complete the statement "I am a(n) _____ reader." Hopefully, your responses will become more positive as you begin to feel more confident about your reading abilities. Believe that your past is not predictive of your future.

You Are Only Human

With all the technological advancements upon us, many people feel pressure to keep pace with the amazing speed and efficiency of computers. But, let's face it, you can't open the top of your head where your processor—your brain—is, add in a computer chip, and announce you are a Pentium. If you had Pentium abilities, you could read almost at the speed of light while storing information in a massive database. "Oh, I read that article in 1991. I'll pull it right up." Sorry, it just isn't going to happen. But don't despair—you can take your horse and buggy brain and make it into a reading race car.

Lack of Reading Training

When *was* the last time you had any training to develop or polish your reading skills? If I were to venture an educated guess based on more than a decade teaching this topic, I would say only about one in twenty people may have taken an additional course, read a book, or followed an audiotape course *in its entirety* for faster reading. If you chuckled when you read the last line, you are probably thinking about the book or tape program you bought years ago that is currently sitting on a shelf half listened to or maybe even unopened. The other nineteen people haven't had any developmental reading training since elementary school.

If you mentally calculate your present age and subtract six, the approximate age you probably began reading, you get the number of years you have been building your current reading skills. For some readers, it's a very long time. I am constantly amazed at how well people learn to adapt to their increased reading workload without any formal training. I have met lawyers, doctors, engineers, financial planners, and other educated professionals who now after all their years of formal education want to learn to read faster. One middle-aged lawyer I met told me he had finally come to a breaking point managing his reading workload. I asked how he made it through his college courses and certification programs without this essential skill. He said he really didn't know, he just did what he had to do. He believed that reading took him a long time, though he had not figured his reading speed or comprehension, and he found himself rereading information frequently because he didn't understand it the first time. He decided it was time to do something about his poor attitude and his sluggish reading style. It's never too late to do something about your creaky reading skills.

Your "To Read" Pile

Everybody has a reading pile—magazines, newspapers, mail, trade journals or other reading material for work, novels, how-to books. Some call it the "to do" stack. I call it the "to read" stack. I sometimes call it the "too high to read" stack. These piles are the visual evidence of the information explosion. Not only do you have an explosion of print material but also a massive amount of information available to read on the Internet. You look at the pile and say, "Oh, forget it. I'm going to recycle the whole batch. I just don't have time."

The good news is you don't need to read it all. You simply need to make a conscious decision regarding what to read carefully, what to skim, and what to disregard. Throughout this book, I will give you information on achieving this goal.

Not Having Enough Time

Since most people today juggle a job, kids, carpool, and a myriad of other responsibilities, they don't have time to read. They put their reading on a pile labeled "later." This "later" pile rarely gets smaller because "later" doesn't come, unless time is made intentionally for it.

In this book, you will learn ways to gain control of your reading workload and to eliminate the dismay when you see the ever growing pile of material.

So, now you possess an opinion of yourself as a reader. You are human and working with antiquated skills. You are living in the midst of a burgeoning information tidal wave and you may not be giving reading enough time. What are you going to do?

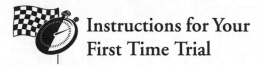

Instructions for Your First Time Trial

Okay, let's hit the road. First you need to find out how you read with regard to speed and comprehension. The following exercise takes less than five minutes to complete. Follow these simple steps and you will begin to better understand who you are as a reader.

1. **Time yourself.** Have a clock or watch with a second hand next to you or a stopwatch or a kitchen timer and time how long it takes to read the passage "All About Reading" below. READ NORMALLY! Write your total time in minutes and seconds in the space provided at the end of the reading.

All About Reading

Think back to the time you were taught to read as a child. First, you learned the alphabet and how letters formed into syllables. Then, how syllables formed into words. Finally, you stood beside your desk and read aloud.

In oral reading, you were forced to read *word by word*. This habit probably carried over into your silent reading. If you are reading a word at a time silently, you read no faster than you speak—150 words per minute.

Forming letters into syllables and then syllables into words leads to the next logical step in reading—forming words into phrases or thought units. Words are symbols for communication that impart their fullest meaning only in association with one another.

Because you learned to read as a child, you are probably trying to meet the adult reading challenge with outdated methods from your elementary school days. Psychologists know that you form your strongest habits during childhood and reading habits are among these. No wonder most of us are not able to keep up.

Ineffective habits are generally characterized by *passive* behaviors, while effective ones require *active* behaviors. By learning to actively read, you read more in less time, improve your concentration, and understand and remember information better.

In the process of reading, your eyes function similarly to a camera. You take a picture of the words you are reading and flash them to your brain. Your brain instantly interprets the meaning of the words.

Actually, while you are reading this, your eyes are stopping about 95 percent of the time. You are not moving your eyes in a smooth flow but rather in jerky stops and starts.

Obviously, then, if you teach your eyes to take larger, or panoramic, pictures at each stop, they will stop less and get more. Larger pictures mean more words are flashed to the brain at each stop and your brain has the capacity to interpret phrases or even whole sentences.

Once you develop a sense of reading rhythm, you can read for longer periods without tiring and get much more meaning per minute.

When you improve your reading, you gain a lifetime of benefits such as being a better conversationalist and a more qualified job applicant. Most of the knowledge you acquire comes from reading, and *knowledge is power!* No other skill you possess contributes so richly toward improving your earning power, giving you pleasure, and allowing you to live a fuller life.

Mark your reading time here: _____ (minutes) _____ (seconds).

2. **Respond to statements.** Immediately answer the following statements to the best of your ability WITHOUT looking back at the reading. That's cheating! Estimate the number of answers you believe are correct and put the number in the blank provided.

Comprehension Statements

Without looking back at the reading passage, respond to the following statements by indicating whether the statement is True (T), False (F), or Not Discussed (N).

_____ 1. The article you have just read was mainly about eye movements.

_____ 2. The most important reason for poor reading is no additional instruction since primary school.

_____ 3. If you are a *word reader*, you are probably reading less than 300 words per minute.

_____ 4. The next logical step in reading is to form words into thought units.

_____ 5. Words are symbols of communication that impart their fullest meaning only in the dictionary.

_____ 6. Inefficient readers read only when they have to.

_____ 7. Keeping up with our reading is difficult because of the information explosion.

_____ 8. While you read, your eyes move in a smooth flow.

_____ 9. If you learn to read more rhythmically, you will read longer without tiring.

_____ 10. Reading faster means reading more at each stop.

Now, estimate how many of these answers you believe you have correct out of ten _____.

3. **Check your responses.** Turn to the Answer Key on page 201. If you have any incorrect, mark the correct

response and return to the reading passage to try to understand where you had a problem.

4. **Figure your comprehension percentage.** Add the total number of correct responses you have and multiply by 10. For example, if you have 5 correct, your comprehension is 50 percent. If you have 8 correct, your comprehension is 80 percent, and if you had 10 correct, give yourself 100 percent. Write your comprehension percent in your Personal Progress chart on page 203.

5. **Figure your Words per Minute.** Look at your reading time and round off the seconds to the nearest 10-second mark. For example, if you read the passage in 2 minutes and 27 seconds, round higher, making your reading time 2 minutes 30 seconds. If you read the passage in 1 minute and 42 seconds, round lower to 1 minute 40 seconds. Turn to the Words per Minute chart on page 207 and find your Words per Minute next to your reading time. Write your Words per Minute in your Personal Progress chart.

6. **Track your Time Trial scores.** Go to your Personal Progress chart and make sure you've recorded your Words per Minute, comprehension percentage, and the date you did the exercise. It's also helpful to document other details such as time of day, any preoccupations, strategies used, and so on. This information will help you understand what works and what doesn't when you read. You will use this chart to track your scores over the next ten days.

What Do Your Numbers Mean?

Your numbers reveal who you are as a reader now. The following gives you a quick view of what your Words per Minute mean:

If your Words per Minute were between:	*Then you are probably a:*
100–200	slow reader
200–300	average reader
300–400	good reader
400–500	above average reader

Slow readers are considered slow because they read at talking speed. A person speaks on average between 100 and 150 words per minute, so reading in this range makes you a "talker." Though you are the quietest person in the world, it has no relationship to your reading. Talkers generally have one of two issues against them: They either move their lips while reading or they mentally whisper, or subvocalize, every single word they read. They're basically hearing their own voice reading to themselves word for word.

Have you ever wondered why you sometimes daydream when someone is talking to you or while you are in class? Well, that's because the person talking to you is speaking an average of 150 words per minute and you can think upward of 400 words per minute. That leaves 250 words per minute looking for something to do. So, if you are not mentally engaged in receiving the information such as a lecture on Charles Dickens's *Great Expectations,* you will daydream . . . a lot!

Slow readers sometimes fall asleep while reading. Unfortunately, our voices when reading silently rarely sound like a hyped radio announcer. They are more like a monotone drone.

Average readers read at about 250 words per minute. You

may be wondering how I know. I keep summary sheets of the classes I teach, which include beginning and ending statistical averages. The participants are generally corporate employees from various levels ranging from administrative and secretarial to managerial and executive. The classes are twelve hours long and have an average of fifteen participants. Using three years' worth of classes, I took all of the beginning averages, which consisted of two separate readings, and averaged them out. The resulting number was 252 words per minute. Most participants had not had any reading training since elementary school.

Average readers mentally whisper what they read but not as much as slow readers. They also think more while reading than a slow reader does.

Good readers may talk a little while they read, but in general to a much lesser degree than slow and average readers.

Above average readers, the few who come to my class without any formal training, are able to figure out on their own what works and what doesn't. They usually don't know strategies by name. However, they are looking to know if what they are doing is right. They are happy to finally have names to attach to their self-made habits so they can continue reading well without guilt.

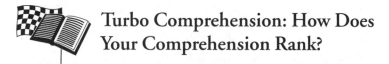 ## Turbo Comprehension: How Does Your Comprehension Rank?

Good comprehension falls between 70 and 90 percent or seven to nine correct responses out of ten. Ten out of ten, or 100 percent, is excellent comprehension, but striving for it on a regular basis is difficult; remember, you're human!

You were asked to guess how many answers you thought you had correct out of ten before checking your answers. I asked you to do this because I have found that many people's perceptions of how many answers they thought they had correct does not match reality. Most *underestimate* their abilities, meaning they get more answers correct than they thought. You see, the brain works in mysterious ways. Many times it works subconsciously without your knowing or feeling secure. But miraculously, you get the right answer. If this happened to you, think about trusting your brain more and believing that you really are capable of better comprehension. In time, you will feel more confident about your comprehension.

Ten Things Your Elementary School Teacher Told You and Your Secondary School Teacher Should Have Told You Not to Do Anymore

1. You have to read every word.
2. You need to sound out every word aloud or in your head.
3. Don't use your hands or fingers to help read.
4. You need to completely understand everything you read.
5. You need to remember everything you read.
6. Go for quantity—the more the better.
7. Don't skim, that's cheating.
8. Don't write in your books.
9. It doesn't matter what you read as long as you read.
10. Speed is not important.

By the end of this book, you will understand why these ten so-called rules are fallacies.

 ## Fast Tracks: Adding a Stick Shift to Your Reading

Many readers are uncomfortable using their hands, or a pen, or a white card to read. Put on the brakes, I'm going to show you how to use these tools.

This approach is based on the fact that your eyes naturally follow movement. If you are in an office talking with someone and a fly is circling in your vicinity, your eyes notice it and momentarily follow it. Or, if you are facing a window where people are walking by, your eyes naturally gravitate toward the foot traffic no matter how riveted you are by your conversation.

Your hand, a pen, or a blank white card, when used to increase your reading speed, are called *pacers*. Think of a pacer as a stick shift. Pacers force the eyes to move in a directed pattern down the page to help you get up to speed.

Pacers function like a pace car in a race. A pace car leads the other cars, or in the case of reading, your eyes and brain, to a speed where the race begins. Once the cars reach a certain speed, the pace car exits the speedway, signaling the start of the race. In reading, your pacer ideally does the same thing: It gets you up to speed, then moves out of the way until you need it again. The pace car returns to the track, getting cars back up to speed if there is an interruption in the race such as an accident or debris on the track. When you read, an interruption could simply be your mind taking a neutral dip in concentration or a sound like the honking of a car horn or the ringing of a telephone. Pacers are helpful in getting you dialed in, which in car racing means your car is perfectly set up for a race.

Each chapter—or day—of this book introduces you to a new pacer. Be aware they may not all work for you—but it's important to try them all and choose those that work best for you.

The general rules to follow when using any pacer are:

1. Keep your pacer moving down, not across the page.

2. Do not stop or go back.

Though rules are meant to be broken, the more you can stick to these two, the better you will read.

 ## Start Your Engines with a White Card

Let's start with our first pacer—the white card method. You need a blank white 3 x 5 index card or the blank side of a business card. Now, if you have ever read with a card before, you most likely place it under the line you are reading. Think about this: Why are you blocking where your eyes are going and leaving open where you have been? This encourages an inefficient, or passive, habit called *regression*, or going back over material you have already read.

So take your white card and place it *on top* of the lines you read, leaving the lane open where you are going. Try this while reading a magazine or newspaper or even this book. As you read, move the card down the page at your own pace. Later when you learn other speed techniques, the card helps you move even faster.

If you tried this and you feel really uncomfortable, don't get rid of it so fast. Day 2 will help you better understand this skill-building process. Know that this discomfort is part of learning.

Pit Stop: Tip of the Day

Before you take things out of your reading pile, you need to know what you are receiving and where it comes from. Take a piece of paper and keep a record of your reading material, including newspapers, magazines, professional journals, newsletters, e-mail newsletters, and so on. Since most publications are issued weekly or monthly, keep the list for one month. Hence, this is called the "One Month Tracker." Then, rate each piece, assessing its value to you and why you should keep it. If you can't come up with a valid reason, cancel your subscription. The ones you don't have time for toss in the recycling bin. Hint: If you have five or more unread back issues of any one publication, chances are you either don't have time for it or do not find value in it. Get rid of it! Day 7 will provide you with more tips on reducing the pileup.

In Day 2, you will discover the parts of your "reading engine." You will gain an understanding about each part and what is involved in the tune-up. Make sure your gas tank is full. Tomorrow is another day on the roadway to faster reading.

Rebuilding Your
Speed Reading Engine

The engine is the core of a race car. When the engine is set up properly, the car is a solid contender in a race. When it's not, and the engine blows, the car is prevented from getting to the next level of competition. In reading, your engine is your eyes and brain. Though your hands are helpful, they are not necessary. (You *can* read a highway road sign without your hands.) Also, your mouth isn't useful, since it slows you down. Remember that when you "talk" while you read you limit yourself to around 150 words per minute.

In this chapter, you will discover the parts of your reading engine, gain an understanding about how they function, and what is involved in tuning up that engine.

Is Your Engine Inefficient or Efficient?

Here is a list of inefficient and efficient reader qualities. Each of these qualities are addressed throughout the book. Review the lists and mark those you recognize as your own current reading habits. Using a pen or pencil, continue marking the lists according to the following example:

- If you read slowly, mark the left side of the "Inefficient Reader" column.
- If you read fast, mark the right side of the "Efficient Reader" column.
- If both qualities describe you, mark the center, between both columns.

Inefficient Reader	Efficient Reader
Reads slowly	Reads rapidly
Has irregular eye movements*	Has rhythmic eye movements*
Understands poorly	Understands well
Uses narrow eye span*	Uses wide eye span*
Reads without a purpose*	Reads with a purpose*
Reads one word at a time	Reads in thought units
Use one reading rate*	Uses varied reading rates*
Believes everything read	Evaluates everything read
Has a limited vocabulary	Has a wide vocabulary
Reads similar kinds of materials	Reads varied materials
Reads infrequently/dislikes reading	Reads frequently/enjoys reading
Has limited background of general knowledge and experience	Has broad background of general knowledge and experience

The Qualities Most Asked About

Some of the above qualities are self-explanatory while others on the list need further explanation. Let's take a look at the characteristics with asterisks and see what they mean.

- **Irregular vs. rhythmic eye movements.** If you think you read one word at a time, or if you get to the end of a line and frequently miss the beginning of the next line, or if you find yourself rereading the same line, then you have more irregular than rhythmic eye movements.

- **Narrow vs. wide eye span.** You have a narrow eye span if you know you read word for word. If you don't read every word or you know you read more than one word at a time, you have a wider eye span. If you want to learn how to read faster, you will need to see more each time your eyes stop, widening your eye span.

- **Reading with vs. without a purpose.** Reading with a purpose means knowing why or for what reason you are reading a certain book, magazine, or letter. It is similar to having a goal in mind. For example, when you read a newspaper you may read with the purpose of staying on top of world or local current events. Reading without a purpose means reading with no goal in mind, like going to a department store and saying "I'm just looking."

- **One reading rate vs. varied reading rates.** If you read your favorite magazine at the same speed you read a school textbook, then you are reading with one reading rate. As an efficient reader you vary your reading rate, or change reading speed, depending on factors such as how much you already know about the content or what you need to learn from the reading.

Inefficient Readers: Passive vs. Active

Inefficient readers are considered passive because they do not do anything while reading to increase speed or comprehension. You may possess some of the inefficient reader qualities because you just haven't been taught how to be efficient. The educators I have worked with are unaware of what they should be teaching to make students efficient readers. No one taught them how.

What, then, is the opposite of passive? Active! Efficient readers activate their conscious mind. They're mindful in their reading and they know how to pull a reading tool out of their hypothetical pocket when needed. It doesn't mean they quickly read through everything, but they find the material mentally engaging and know how to get the most out of it, quickly.

Efficient Readers: Effective vs. Efficient

Please do not confuse effective and efficient, however. Effective reading simply means you read with satisfactory comprehension. For example, a twenty-five-page chapter of a textbook can take you three hours to read. If you understand it, then you're reading effectively. If you don't grasp the content, you're reading it ineffectively. Efficient reading means you understand it the first time, read with good comprehension, and *in less time*. That same twenty-five-page chapter read efficiently can be read in half the time while still being effective.

The Three Passive Habits for Losing the Reading Race

The most common passive reading habits are mind wandering, regression, and subvocalization. They prevent you from reaching the finish line efficiently. *You cannot get rid of any of them, only reduce them.* Becoming aware of them is the first step to improving your chances of winning.

Mind Wandering

Mind wandering is also known as daydreaming. All readers do it but active readers do it less than passive ones. Mind wandering while reading is effective if you are mentally applying what you are reading to something you already know. For example, if you took a trip to Italy several years ago and you're reading a magazine article about Italian art preservation activities, your mind most likely wanders to your trip. You mentally relate what you personally experienced with the information presented in the article. This is what I call *active* mind wandering because this is how you learn. You build bridges of knowledge from what you know to the new material on the page.

I use a concept called *brain glue*. Everything you have learned and experienced is your brain glue. When you stretch it and stick new information to it, then you are active. If you wallow in it without stretching or adding to it, then you are passive.

Passive mind wandering is thinking about a million other unrelated tasks or plans, such as remembering to make a vet appointment, or thinking about an upcoming party, or thinking about _____. You fill in the blank!

Too much passive mind wandering slows you down, prevents you from getting better comprehension skills, and wastes your time. If you want to edge closer toward the winner's circle, then you need to reduce your passive mind wandering.

Regression

Regression is a flick of your eyes back to a word or words previously read. For example, if you have ever arrived at the bottom of a page wondering what you just read, you are forced to regress to the top. Many people unconsciously flick their eyes backward as they read forward. If you frequently get sleepy while reading, even while sitting upright at a desk or table, chances are your eyes are regressing a lot.

As with mind wandering, there is active and passive regression. Active regression is intentionally going back looking for what you missed. You are reading consciously but you don't quite get the author's meaning. Sometimes, for example, you need to go back after you come across a word you don't know. You go back with a purpose in mind.

Passive regression is when you go back and reread words or passages because your mind is wandering or your concentration is off. Many people simply do not trust their brain when reading. This insecurity creates a situation ripe for passive regression. They feel they have to double back while reading to make sure they understand the content. It's similar to watching a movie. Most times you hear everything said but sometimes you miss its meaning or you thought you heard incorrectly. If you are watching at home on your VCR, you take the remote and rewind (regress) to hear it again. If you are in a movie theater, you cannot rewind the film. You have to trust that either you heard correctly or that you'll figure it out from the rest of the movie's context (and you usually do).

When participants in my classes begin to use the white card method, they become acutely aware of their previous need to reread. This awareness, coupled with the white card method, begins the reduction of passive regression. You can try this, too.

Subvocalization

Subvocalization means mentally reading word for word or physically moving your lips while reading. If your beginning reading rate on Day 1 was under two hundred words per minute, then you are subvocalizing. Look at your Personal Progress chart on page 203. If you read at a greater speed you may also be subvocalizing but just not as much. Remember you cannot get rid of this voice, only reduce it.

There are some occasions when the talking is active. For example, hearing your voice repeat or say the information to yourself while you are studying or memorizing is active. When you read poetry or dialogue, such as from a play, you need to hear the rhythm and intonation to truly appreciate these forms of writing. Students tell me—and I agree—that reading the Bible or Shakespeare is challenging without mentally talking. As far as your brain is concerned, it finds it as challenging as trying to read a foreign language. I also suggest reading the fine print of legal and insurance documents word for word unless you are a lawyer or insurance agent who is familiar with the jargon.

Though you may have a good reason to subvocalize, remember that it slows you down. Keep this in mind when you plan your reading time.

So, unless you're reading *Hamlet* or memorizing poetry, the talking is passive and therefore slows you down. Many readers believe that when they read something for the first time, they must study or memorize it. I believe this is another remnant of your school days. How can you study or memorize something when you don't even know what it is about? You will learn a powerful technique called *pre-viewing* on Day 5, which will help you discover what the reading is about *before* you begin.

Ten Ways to Reduce the Talking

Talking while reading, either by moving your lips while reading or mentally whispering every word, slows you down.

Everyone does it, but efficient readers do it less. Here are ten proven strategies to help you reduce the talking:

1. **Catch yourself doing it.** Only when you realize you are talking can you do something about it.

2. **Read faster!** This is by far the best strategy. The faster you read, the less you can talk word for word.

3. **Read key words.** This naturally helps you reduce the talking, since you are only speaking the key words.

4. **Use a pacer.** Each day you will learn a new pacer technique. Whichever one you choose will help you read faster and reduce the talking.

5. **Hush it.** Press your index finger to your lips while you read as if you were telling a child to be quiet. Put your finger to your mouth anytime you feel yourself talking.

6. **Mumble.** Try saying something like "1-2-3, 1-2-3" or "la-la-la" to yourself while reading silently.

7. **Hum.** Hum a tune to yourself while reading silently.

8. **Chew gum.** Try chewing three or more pieces at a time. While reading, use a rhythmic chewing motion.

9. **Put toothpaste on your lips.** If you move your lips while reading, you will taste the toothpaste and it will remind you to stop talking.

10. **Silence your tongue.** Press your tongue to the roof of your mouth to reduce your talking.

 Time Trial No. 2

Okay, buckle your seat belt. It's time to evaluate your engine. The following exercise takes less than five minutes to complete.

The following passage gives you the opportunity to experiment with the white card pacer. While reading, be aware of your daydreaming, regressing, or mental talking. Notice whether these habits are active or passive.

1. **Time yourself.** See how long it takes to read the passage "Battling the Worry Bug" below. Write your total time in minutes and seconds in the space provided at the end of the reading.

Battling the Worry Bug

By John D. Whitman

Worrying is good. Worrying to a degree is even healthy. From an evolutionary point of view, it's probably the human ability to worry that got us where we are today. Since early human beings were generally unable to outrun or outfight larger, faster, sharper-clawed animals, our ability to anticipate danger played a role in our survival as a species.

Unfortunately, while times have changed, our instincts haven't. The majority of humans have far fewer immediate physical threats or concerns than their ancestors (how many of you are, at this moment, worried about being eaten by a cave bear?). But according to several studies, the worry level of average Americans is increasing. At its most intense, this type of chronic worrying qualifies as an anxiety disorder.

Researchers identify this syndrome as GAD, or general anxiety disorder. Studies suggest that GAD afflicts about one in twenty adults during some point in their lives. Why are some people prone to anxiety while the rest of us cruise along humming "Don't worry, be happy"? Scientists point to many factors.

Apparently, some of us are born worriers. Researchers at the Medical College of Virginia estimate that the tendency to worry can be genetically inherited. Those who aren't born worriers can develop the tendency during childhood, either by an unsettling event or the demands of overprotective parents who give their children the impression that everything is worth worrying about.

A related factor is an early assignment of responsibility. In one study, almost two thirds of GAD sufferers stated that as children they were given adult responsibilities, such as caring for younger siblings. They learned that in order to receive love they had to watch out for every real or imagined threat.

The upshot of GAD is that worrying becomes a self-fulfilling prophecy. As the brain worries more, it loses the ability to distinguish real problems from nonproblems.

How to break the worry cycle? Therapists help worriers develop methods to identify moments when they worry. For example, one patient wore a rubber band on her wrist and snapped it every time she found herself worrying. Raising sufferers' self-awareness of their mental attitudes helps them distinguish between when they worry about real problems, or when they are simply worrying for worry's sake.

No therapist will tell you that curing worrywarts is a snap, but such effective therapies give us hope that GAD isn't something we have to worry about.

Mark your reading time here: _____ (minutes) _____ (seconds).

2. **Respond to statements.** Immediately answer the following statements to the best of your ability WITHOUT looking back at the reading. Estimate the number of answers you believe are correct and put the number in the blank provided.

Comprehension Statements

Without looking back at the reading passage, respond to the following statements by indicating whether the statement is True (T), False (F), or Not Discussed (N).

_____ 1. GAD stands for genetic anxiety disease.

_____ 2. Studies suggest about one in twenty people are affected by GAD sometime in their lives.

_____ 3. Worrying is a human instinct dating as far
            back as the caveman days.

_____ 4. More women than men worry.

_____ 5. Worriers are never born that way.

_____ 6. The tendency to worry can develop as a result
            of giving a child adult responsibilities at an
            early age.

_____ 7. The more a person worries, the less the brain
            can distinguish nonproblems from real prob-
            lems.

_____ 8. More and more people are choosing to partici-
            pate in anxiety research.

_____ 9. E-GAD is the term used for extreme worriers.

_____ 10. There are effective therapies for GAD sufferers.

Now, estimate how many of these answers you believe you
have correct out of ten _____.

3. **Check your responses.** Turn to the Answer Key on page
    201. If you have any incorrect, mark the correct
    response and return to the reading passage to try to
    understand where you had a problem.

4. **Figure your comprehension percentage.** Add the total
    number of correct responses you have and multiply by
    10. Write your comprehension percentage in your
    Personal Progress chart on page 204.

5. **Figure your Words per Minute.** Look at your reading
    time and round off the seconds to the nearest 10-second
    mark. Turn to the Words per Minute chart on page 207
    and find your Words per Minute next to your reading
    time. Write your Words per Minute in your Personal
    Progress chart.

6. **Track your Time Trial scores.** Go to your Personal Progress chart and make sure you've recorded your Words per Minute, comprehension percentage, and the date you did the exercise. It's also helpful to document other details such as time of day, any preoccupations, strategies used, and so on.

A Guaranteed Solution for Becoming a Race Contender

One of the best ways to reduce mind wandering, regression, and subvocalization is—to read faster. By increasing your speed, your brain has less time to daydream. You are filling it with more words—remember the 150-words-per-minute talker vs. the 400-words-per-minute thinker?—leaving your brain less time to wander off. Your tendency to regress is reduced. And reading faster naturally reduces the mental whispering because you simply cannot read word for word when you are increasing your reading speed.

 ## Fast Tracks: The Process of Retooling the Engine

You will be happy to know that it is possible to take a poor reading engine and replace it with better parts to make it purr like a kitten. That's what you're about to do. You are going to replace some passive habits with active ones.

You might have tried to read faster on your own without any formal training. Perhaps because you had a lot to read in a short period or just because you wanted to try. You probably discovered that though you read faster, you missed a lot of the meaning. And at that time you probably said to yourself, "What's the point? Why read faster if I don't understand it?"

You were actually coming to the part of retooling where people run into trouble. In the process of trying to upgrade your skills, you begin working with a new set of strategies. Ironically, instead of getting instantly better, you initially get worse. This is what I call "unlearning to relearn." However, over time, with perseverance and repetition, your skills improve.

A perfect analogy is driving an automatic car as opposed to a stick shift. Let's say that you only drive an automatic car. As sometimes happens, your car breaks down. It will take at least a week to repair. You absolutely positively have to get to work for a big meeting. Your neighbor says, "You can use my car," and it's a stick shift. Now, I know some of you are thinking, "I'd rather carpool or rent a car, anything to avoid a stick shift," but just stay with me.

You take the keys, get behind the wheel of the car, put the key in the ignition, and all of a sudden driving isn't the same anymore. For starters, when you turn the key, the car lurches forward and stalls. You don't know that you have to put your foot on the clutch—a third pedal—in order to stop the car from moving. To make matters worse you also have a stick shift with five numbers and the letter R staring at you. Putting the car in reverse is now very tricky.

Let's stop here to answer a few questions. Are you a bad driver or just an unskilled operator? Are you comfortable or uncomfortable? Are you confident or insecure? If you drive the stick shift for several days, do you think you would feel more comfortable? Probably. Would you make better time on the second day than the first day? Most likely. After a few days, might you feel more confident in your abilities? I can assure you that by the end of the week, you will feel more willing and confident to drive while drinking a coffee or making a call using a cell phone. In the beginning, relearning a skill you already have is frustrating and challenging. If you stick it out and continue to figure out what works and what doesn't through trial and error, you will build the skills you are trying to improve.

What Your Eyes Do When You Read

Find a partner who can help you with this quick exercise. Don't be shy about asking but if no one is around, you can do it later. One of you will take on the role of the silent reader while the other will be the observer. The reader should face the observer. The reader needs to select anything to read. This book is just fine or grab something from your "read later" pile. The reader then lifts the material up to just below eye height, so the observer can see the reader's eyeballs. The reader then reads silently for about thirty seconds while the observer watches the reader's eye movements. When you're done, switch roles with your partner.

What might you see? A process similar to a typewriter. You see small jerky movements going across a line and you might imagine a quiet "ding"—as typewriters used to do before computers—when the reader reaches the end of the line before going on to the beginning of the next line.

What you really see is the eyes *stopping* and *jumping*. Your eyes stop and jump on average every quarter of a second, or four times per second. You read, or pick up information, only when you stop. Each jump takes you from one stop to the next. And what your eyes see in one eye stop is your *eye span*. Remember the narrow vs. wide eye span discussed earlier? If you want to learn how to read faster, you need to see more each time your eyes stop, widening your eye span.

What's on the Side of Your Road?

You can widen your eye span and therefore read faster because of peripheral vision. This is your visual boundary or what you can see on the left and right while looking straight ahead. Though the outer area of your boundary is blurry, the inner part—the part you see when you stare directly ahead—is focused.

There are two quick ways to assess your peripheral vision ability. Both methods require your eyes and your hands.

- **Method 1: Finding your peripheral vision breaking point.** Stare at something directly in front of you. Raise your arms straight out in front of you at shoulder height and point your fingertips toward the ceiling. Slowly move your hands and arms apart to either side *without moving your head or your eyes.* Your hands are not in focus but they are visible. When you are at the point where you no longer see your hands, since they are now too far out of your periphery, bring them back in just enough to where you can see them again. Now, look at how far apart your hands are. This is your peripheral vision ability.

- **Method 2: Discovering your eye span.** Choose a letter in the center of a line of text and place a finger on the left and right of it. Stare directly at the letter without moving your eyes or head. Slowly move your fingers apart, exposing more letters and words. Look at how much you see while still focusing on the letter. This is your present eye span ability. With practice, you can widen your eye span.

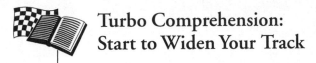 ## Turbo Comprehension: Start to Widen Your Track

In Day 4, you will learn how to widen your eye span with two specific strategies: reading key words and reading phrases. But right now you can get a jump start on learning to widen your eye span.

The Eye Span Pyramid

Focus carefully on the number at the center of each line. Start with the top number and slowly jump your eyes to stop on the next number down. By focusing hard you will see the numbers or syllables at both ends simultaneously. It will be more challenging as you go down. Come back to this from time to time to gauge your peripheral vision ability.

4 1 6

26 2 57

44 3 60

38 4 16

92 5 11

47 6 15

81 7 66

94 8 12

80 9 28

	j	l	r
	ad	2	bo
	be	3	to
	ko	4	gr
	fit	5	mop
	lo	6	is
	fa	7	ti
	fun	8	jan
	it	9	tip

Phrase Flashing

This exercise is designed to help you develop a quick and accurate perception of phrases as thought groups. It also serves as an introduction to a faster reading technique called *phrasing*. The objective of this exercise is to glance at each phrase, completely reading the phrase as a whole.

With a blank 3 x 5 index card in your hand, cover the column of phrases. Then with a quick flick of your wrist, move the card down to reveal just one line and immediately back up again to cover the phrase. This exposes the first phrase of the column for an instant. Keep the rest of the column covered. Predict what you believe you saw by saying it aloud or writing it down. If you're not sure, take a guess. Then check yourself by uncovering the phrase or column. Quickly move down each column, repeating the procedure for each line. Return to this exercise from time to time to retest your skill. Keep track of how many phrases you get correct by putting the number at the bottom of each set.

Set 1	Set 2
a success story	her purple dress
more and more	strange question
get out of hand	old acquaintance
the grim reaper	forever and ever
as they do say	now and again
once and for all	lead him to dance
the other one	not my fair share
bright and early	incidentally
being in fashion	do the impossible
six months ago	the nurse practitioner
notwithstanding	musical revue
before and after	as clear as crystal
what time is it?	old as the hills
better than ever	an optical illusion
in the meantime	bacteriological
free information	the spare tire
finished product	out on strike
beyond question	add to the mix
the spare tires	take to the party
our way of life	telecommuter

Number correct out
of twenty: _____.

Number correct out
of twenty: _____.

The more phrases correct out of twenty, the less help you need with this technique. However, if you didn't do well, there are other ways to improve. For example, the next time you are at a light or stuck in traffic look at the license plate in front of you and then quickly look away. Can you accurately predict what you just saw? Also try this with road signs, billboards, or writing on the sides of trucks.

An Important Word About Your Brain

Your eyes act as a window to your brain. If you have been an untrained, passive reader, your eyes have been open only a crack. In the process of learning to read faster, your eye muscles have to stretch in order to get more information to the brain in a shorter amount of time. Initially, your brain will have a difficult time handling the extra load. You can almost hear it say, "Whoa! What are you doing? I'm not used to all this information at once!"

Find comfort in the fact that your brain is constantly seeking meaning for everything it registers. It is always looking to comprehend even though at times you may not think so. It takes the brain a little time to figure out what your eyes are doing and, before long, your comprehension is back, or even better than before.

 ## Start Your Engines: The Left Side Pull

In Day 1, I described the reasons and uses of "Adding a Stick Shift to Your Reading." You might want to go back to this section to refresh your memory about pacers. Initially, you may experience some natural discomfort as you adjust to using each pacer but with practice it will become more comfortable.

When trying the eye span flashing exercise earlier in this chapter, you might have noticed that you were more accurate on the left side than the right. This is because you have learned to read left to right.

The Left Side Pull—today's new pacer—helps you focus your eyes on the beginning of the line as well as keep your place reading down the text. Choose a page in a magazine, newspaper, or this book to experiment with. With an empty hand, either left or right, point your index finger next to the left side, or beginning of the line. As you read across a line, slowly but continually move your finger down the left side of the column. As you get more accustomed to using it, try moving it a little faster.

Gauge Your Attitude

Let's take an attitude check. Write down or mentally fill in the blank of the following statement:

I am a(n) _____ reader.

Is your reading attitude changing?

 ## Pit Stop: Tip of the Day

If you are like most people, you have no idea how much time you actually spend reading on a daily or a weekly basis. You may know, however, by looking at your piles that you need more time. To really make use of the information in this book, you need time to read and experiment with the new techniques. Otherwise they won't work for you. It doesn't mean you have to read a specific amount every day. It doesn't mean you need to spend hours at a time. You probably read every day. Think about it. You read your mail. You check your e-mail. You peruse memos, reports, textbooks, newspapers, or magazines. You can use these times to practice without making any extra time to read. Whatever you do, you need to figure out when you can fit in more practice reading.

Look at your schedule. Decide when you can add a little

reading to your day or use your current reading time to experiment. Be flexible with the time. Just do it!

Day 3 will focus on learning how to improve your concentration, which is one of the most important skills to reading quickly with better comprehension.

Revving Up Your Concentration

Concentration is the art of being focused, the ability to pay attention. Unskilled readers try hard to concentrate but frequently daydream instead. This is especially true when reading nonfiction, or factual material, such as most work materials and textbooks.

According to Becky Patterson, author of *Concentration: Strategies for Attaining Focus*, there are five basic reasons why concentration is important, especially while reading. Concentration helps you:

1. **Function more productively in a fast-paced world.** Our lives are busier, our options more plentiful, and our time increasingly more precious. Without the ability to concentrate, we fall into the trap of trying to balance a dozen things in our mind at the same time or staying so busy that we don't even notice we are not moving forward.

2. **Emulate an important characteristic of successful people.** Successful people have learned to shut out

everything and zero in on a single task such as reading or running a meeting or making a phone call.

3. **Improve the quality of your life.** Think about it: How much of your reading time do you spend thinking about the past and the future? Is your present going by unnoticed? Learning to focus on the present is the best way to live life to the fullest.

4. **Accomplish more in less time.** If you focus while you read, you will spend less time than if you spend your time passively daydreaming.

5. **Tap into a deep reservoir of energy.** When you are really concentrating, you don't feel hunger, fatigue, or boredom. Instead you are filled with energy and don't place limits on yourself.

Do you think you are fully concentrating right now? If so, what is enabling you to do so? If not, what is distracting you? How can you develop *more* concentration? The answers to these questions are the focus of this chapter.

Dialing In to Concentration

A car racing team's expertise is preparing the car for a race. The process of dialing in means doing a series of activities, not just one, including tuning up the engine, changing the oil, checking the tire pressure, and so on. Lack of focus from anyone on the race team could mean losing the race.

In reading, there are many conditions that create concentration. However, there are just as many or more that derail it. You are ultimately responsible for setting up the appropriate conditions for achieving the highest level of concentration.

Let's learn how to create concentration while reading by

becoming aware of what distracts you and taking control over these distractions.

Choosing What to Read

If you have a week's vacation coming up, you have several things to think about, such as where you want to go and why, how you are going to get there, and what you want to do.

Just as you would mentally prepare yourself for your vacation, you also need to prepare your mind for reading. This is the first step for ensuring concentration and reading efficiency. The two most powerful questions you can ask yourself before you read are:

1. "**WHY** am I reading this?" and

2. "**WHAT** might I need this information for?"

Your answers to these questions help you uncover your *purpose* and *responsibility*. Before I read, I have a mental conversation with every piece of reading material. For example, let's say that the next item on my reading pile is a professional journal. I place it in my hand, look over the cover, and mentally ask, "Why am I reading this?" If I cannot come up with a valid reason, I choose not to read it. If I'm not sure, I open it and quickly scan the Table of Contents. If I see an article I'm interested in, I again ask the question "Why would I read it?" I mentally answer the question. For example, I am reading this "to enhance my knowledge" or "to keep abreast of current world affairs." You will come up with additional reasons if you remember to ask yourself the *why* question before you read.

Once you identify your purpose, then think about your responsibility. "What might I need this information for?" or

"What might I use this information for?" For example, I need this information "for a test," "for a meeting," "to sell my prospect," "to help my child do better in school," and so on.

Many of my workshop participants have told me they are so amazed when they take the time to consciously decide their reading purpose and responsibility. They say that they save a lot of time by reading only what they find useful to them. They also find that their attention is focused, which helps with comprehension.

 ## Fast Tracks: Where Do You Read?

Think about the place you most often read. In your mind, visualize how it looks. Take a blank piece of paper, any size will do, and draw a rough sketch of the location. Include everything in the space such as a computer, TV, chairs, telephone, stereo, doorway, window, garbage can, and so on.

When you complete your sketch, place an X in the picture where you usually sit in the room. Then circle or highlight anything in the room that distracts you from reading. Review the list of distracters below and see how many you identify with when you read.

The Top Ten Reading Distracters

Here is a list of the common reading distracters complied from my workshop participants. Becoming aware of what steers you off track while reading is another step in ensuring better concentration. You may want to place a check mark next to those that apply to you.

1. **Other people.** Whether you work in an office or are at home with your kids, you can be sure that other people will distract you. If you get interrupted, you lose your concentration, you forfeit reading time, you lose your place. If you are interrupted regularly, you probably become stressed and frustrated, making it even more difficult to concentrate on your reading.

2. **Telephone.** If you have roommates or teenage kids, the telephone will ring frequently. If you are at work or home alone, constantly having to stop and answer the phone will interrupt your reading time.

3. **E-mail.** If your computer is programmed to automatically notify you that you have new messages either with music or an instant message, it interrupts and distracts your reading time.

4. **Faxes.** The telephone, e-mail, and faxes have all become what I call "twitch factors." It means that when your phone rings, or your e-mail dings, or your fax chimes, your brain twitches. For many, this happens frequently throughout the day, making for repetitive twitching. It is one thing to be aware of an incoming communication. It is another to stop what you are doing to attend to it.

5. **Music.** For many adults, listening to music is not something they generally do when they read, mainly because they find that as they get older, they have less tolerance for noise in their reading environment. Teenagers are a different story. They are convinced that they can concentrate while listening to loud music with words. Music with words, however, is especially distracting because it reduces the number of words the brain can process while reading. It slows you down.

6. **Television.** If you are trying to watch TV while reading for school or work, what happens? Do you focus more on the reading or the television set? Some people read during commercial breaks, allowing maybe eight minutes per half hour to read. Since television is visual and auditory, you're left with no other senses with which to read.

7. **Location is too comfortable.** To read for pleasure, where do you like to be? On a comfy couch, in a cozy recliner, or a warm bed? When you read for work or for school, are you in any of these places? Your brain is conditioned to relax on a couch, in a recliner, or in bed and to work at a desk or table. If you are trying to work in a place the brain expects to relax, you spend more time reading less.

8. **Not interested in the material.** If your reading material doesn't grab your attention, your mind wanders to wishing you didn't have to read that boring piece of material. Unfortunately, there are times, especially for work or school, when you must read things that are not of interest to you.

9. **Being preoccupied.** It is difficult to read when your brain is full of other goings-on. Just as you cannot squeeze any more data onto an already full computer screen, you cannot add to a full brain.

10. **Reading at the wrong time of day.** Everyone can name a time or times of day when concentration is easier. Some people are morning people. They are more productive and focused during the early hours of the day. Some are night owls who concentrate at night, sometimes very late at night. As important as it is to know what time of day you are most alert, it is also important to know when you are least alert. Adults

returning to school find that they end up doing their
schoolwork late at night after a full day of work and
family responsibilities. If this is not their ideal time of
day to read, they spend more time reading with less
understanding. They may find it more effective to set
their alarm earlier and read before work.

Getting on the Focus Track

For all of the distracters, there are some commonsense solutions for getting and staying on track depending on your situation.

1. **Squirrel yourself away.** Businesspeople can use an open
   conference room or an empty office to get away from
   other people as well as their own phones and computers.
   If you have a door to your office or room, close it.
   Students can go to the library or use an empty
   classroom to find quiet time. Parents at home could
   swap time with another parent by scheduling
   alternating play dates.

2. **Let technology work for you.** Telephone machines and
   voice mail are meant to take messages for you when you
   are unavailable to take the calls. Decide how often and
   when you will check your messages. You can program
   most e-mail software programs to check for messages at
   designated times. Try starting with three times a day.
   Putting yourself on a schedule gives you freedom to
   concentrate on other tasks.

3. **Let others work for you.** To get some uninterrupted
   quiet time, see if you might be able to swap phone
   answering duty with a co-worker or housemate so you
   each get some time. If you are a student working at

home or in your dorm room, tell the other residents to hold your calls and take messages until a certain time when you think you will be done.

4. **Listen to Mozart.** It has been suggested that Mozart's music or any classical music boosts concentration and retention while reading and learning. Play it quietly in the background even when you work to focus your brain on the tasks at hand. It can also be very relaxing, a feeling many need while working. If Mozart is not your style, listen to music without words or with a soothing beat. Some New Age piano or guitar can work well. Just make sure it doesn't become a distracter.

5. **Move to a more appropriate location.** If you want to increase your chances of reading more quickly with better concentration—and ultimately better comprehension and retention—then sit at a desk or table. These are places at which the brain has been conditioned to work.

6. **Turn off the TV.** Perhaps you can flip through a popular magazine, not a professional journal, while watching TV, but to read with serious purpose and responsibility, you should reject the TV as a companion to reading.

7. **Read at your peak time(s) of day.** If you know you are most productive and focused first thing in the morning, then find a way to incorporate reading at that time. Students can help themselves by not reading at night, but instead going to bed earlier and getting up earlier the next day. You will read faster, learn more, and remember what you read better. Adjust your reading schedule to meet your body's natural rhythm.

8. **Brain dump.** If you are about to read (or work) and you have a lot on your mind, write down what you are thinking about. If you are concerned that you will forget to call someone, make a note about it. If you are thinking about an upcoming event you need to be ready for, write down what you need to do. Carry paper and pen with you at all times. You never know when you'll remember something you don't want to forget. Also trust that your subconscious usually finds a way to solve your problem when you are not focusing on it.

9. **Set a time goal.** Give yourself a realistic time limit for reading. By saying you only have a certain amount of time to complete your reading, then you have a better chance of doing it with less daydreaming.

10. **Take short breaks.** Contrary to popular thought, you do not need long periods of time to read. You should be able to get through a daily newspaper in as little as five minutes or as long as thirty. Remember it depends on your purpose and responsibility. However, if you have a lot of reading to do, like college students or business professionals, then you will need to read for longer periods of time now and then.

Reading for long periods of time without resting your eyes and brain can cause burnout. If race car drivers didn't stop during a race, they would run out of gas and wear out their tires, too. Quick breaks are essential for making it through a race. Race car drivers go into a pit lane for refueling, making adjustments, changing worn tires, and so on. The longer the race, the more breaks they have to take. Though it takes time, it is well worth the effort for getting to the finish line efficiently.

Many drivers pit when a yellow caution flag is waved.

This is when the race naturally slows down due to an accident or debris on the track. When you read, you could plan a short break for when you naturally feel your concentration waning. Research shows that concentration can last for only an average of twenty minutes while reading, so you might want to take a quick break, about five minutes, every twenty to thirty minutes. Try not to wait longer than an hour for a break. The shorter the break, the less time you lose and the easier it is to get back up to speed.

By implementing some or all of these suggestions, it will take you less time to read more with better comprehension and retention. You will also immediately reduce passive mind wandering.

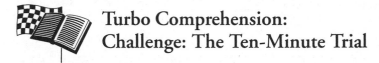 ## Turbo Comprehension: Challenge: The Ten-Minute Trial

When people tell me that they can read efficiently when they watch television, listen to loud music, or eat lunch, I suggest they try the ten-minute trial to test their perception of reality.

- **Step 1.** Take some material you have to read. Read it in your usual place under your usual conditions for ten minutes. If you always have a lively radio station on, make sure it is on. If you always eat while you read or have the television on, continue to do so. At the end of the ten minutes, write down how many pages you read, what you think you read about without looking back at the pages you read, and what, if anything, your mind wandered to.

- **Step 2.** Now make some changes in your reading environment, either physical or mental. You might change your music to a classical station, turn off the television, or refrain from eating. Using the same material, try reading again for another ten minutes. Write down how many pages you read, what you think you read about without looking back at the pages you read, and what, if anything, your mind wandered to.

- **Step 3.** Ask yourself, "Which conditions allow me to read more and/or understand more?" Initially you may be distracted from a lack of your distraction. But in the end decide which conditions have the best chance of helping you increase your reading concentration. You have the power to fully concentrate no matter the circumstances.

 ## Time Trial No. 3

Now is a good time to test your engine. The following exercise takes less than five minutes to complete. Using the ideas presented in "Getting on the Focus Track," set yourself up in an environment most conducive for your concentration.

In the following practice reading, you will have the opportunity to experiment with the white card pacer (see Day 1) or Left Side Pull (see Day 2). While reading, be aware of your daydreaming, regressing, or mental talking. Continue to notice whether you do these habits actively or passively.

1. **Time Yourself.** See how long it takes to read the passage "A True Athlete" below. Write your total time in minutes and seconds in the space provided at the end of the reading.

A True Athlete

By John D. Whitman

One of the most moving and emotional aspects of sporting events is the chance for an athlete to become, for a moment, superhuman.

That comment doesn't refer to weight lifters hefting never-before-achieved weights, or high jumpers clearing bars at new heights. Some of sports' greatest moments happen regardless of the number of goals or the speed of the winner. They happen when one player meets an impossible challenge.

These moments are so incredible, so perfect, that if they were written into fictional stories no one would believe them.

One of the greatest of these athletes is Michael Jordan, the former star of basketball's Chicago Bulls. Jordan's career is one long list of high scores, heroic moments, and highlight films. He led his team to six championships in the 1990s.

Fans and announcers alike speculated that 1998 would be Jordan's last season. That year, Jordan carried the Bulls to yet another championship series. They faced the Utah Jazz, a team that had beaten them during all regular season games.

Following Jordan's lead, the Bulls took control of the first few games of the series. Although they led the series 3–2 at the start of Game 6, momentum shifted to the Jazz, thanks to their All-Star power forward Karl Malone.

But the Bulls had Jordan, and he did not like to lose. In the final moments of a career full of magical moments, he proceeded to orchestrate a series of moves that would epitomize all his achievements.

He scored a lay-up with 37 seconds left that cut the lead to 86–85. Then, as Malone tried to take position near the basket, Jordan snuck around him and stole the ball. Dribbling downcourt, the superstar hesitated for a moment as guard Bryon Russell blocked him. Jordan leaned to his left, then turned back to his right, faking Russell almost onto his hands and knees. Open for a split second, Jordan shot the ball with 5.2 seconds left. The ball hit nothing but the bottom of the net as it sailed through the basket, placing the Bulls into the lead. The Bulls won the game, and took their sixth championship.

It seemed like too much to ask: a great player at the end of a great career, summoning all his skills for one final moment of superhuman effort. But the sports world expects greatness from athletes, and Michael Jordan literally rose to the occasion.

Mark your reading time here: _____ (minutes) _____ (seconds).

2. **Respond to statements.** Immediately answer the following statements to the best of your ability WITHOUT looking back at the reading. Estimate the number of answers you believe are correct and put the number in the blank provided.

Comprehension Statements

Without looking back at the reading passage, respond to the following statements by indicating whether the statement is True (T), False (F), or Not Discussed (N).

_____   1. Some of the greatest moments in sports happen when an athlete meets a seemingly impossible challenge.

_____   2. Michael Jordan played for the Detroit Bulls.

_____   3. Before joining the Bulls, Michael Jordan played for the Utah Jazz.

_____   4. Michael Jordan led his team to four team championships.

_____   5. Despite Michael Jordan's strong playing, the Bulls lost the first few games of the 1998 championship series.

_____   6. Michael Jordan retired because he wanted to spend more time with his family.

_____   7. In the last championship game, Bryon Russell
              fouled out as Jordan dribbled down the court.

_____   8. Michael Jordan is considered a super-athlete
              because he also plays professional baseball.

_____   9. Despite playing on opposing teams, Karl Ma-
              lone and Michael Jordan are good friends.

_____   10. Michael Jordan put superhuman effort into
              the final moments of the last game of his ca-
              reer.

Now, estimate how many of these answers you have correct
out of ten _____.

3. **Check your responses.** Turn to the Answer Key on page
   201. If you have any incorrect, mark the correct
   response and return to the reading passage to try to
   understand where you had a problem.

4. **Figure your comprehension percentage.** Add the total
   number of correct responses you have and multiply by
   10. Write your comprehension percentage in your
   Personal Progress chart on page 204.

5. **Figure your Words per Minute.** Look at your reading
   time and round off the seconds to the nearest 10-second
   mark. Turn to the Words per Minute chart on page 207
   and find your Words per Minute next to your reading
   time. Write your Words per Minute in your Personal
   Progress chart.

6. **Track your Time Trial scores.** Go to your Personal
   Progress chart and make sure you've recorded your
   Words per Minute, comprehension percentage, and the
   date you did the exercise. It's also helpful to document
   other details such as time of day, any preoccupations,
   strategies used, and so on.

Focus with a Pen in Hand

Just when you thought you knew all there was to know about creating concentration while reading, here's another set of strategies. These we'll call the Note Making Tools. They are meant to help you mindfully locate and document the most useful material in any reading. They should not always be used because they can waste your time, especially if your purpose doesn't warrant it or you aren't going to need the information again. The Note Making Tools can be used when you want or need to:

1. Refer to the information again, or
2. Quickly locate one piece of information, such as a quote or statistic.

Using a Highlighter Effectively

When it comes to using a highlighter, most people do not use it effectively. They use the highlighter as a coloring tool. They locate a paragraph they want to highlight, which is an active reading process, and proceed to cover each line with their colored highlighter. Then they may notice some white space between the lines, and proceed to fill in the color. Finally they see that the color is ragged on the edges, so they smooth out the edges, making a colored box out of the highlighted paragraph. This has now become a passive activity.

This *coloring activity* is *very distracting* and a *waste of time.* This is because this type of *highlighting postpones learning.* If you need to learn the information in the paragraph for a test, then you would be using highlighting inefficiently. You will eventually *have to reread* the whole paragraph, trying *to decide why you highlighted* it in the *first place!*

If you want to highlight efficiently, then *only highlight the key words.* Rarely should you highlight more than a phrase. Key words for highlighting are the words that have the most meaning in the sentence or paragraph. Now go back to the last paragraph and read only the italicized words for an example of efficient highlighting.

If you feel you need to highlight an entire paragraph, use margin notes instead (see next section). The only time you should highlight an entire paragraph is when you have to document a quote. But generally you don't ever need to highlight a whole sentence or a whole paragraph.

Creating Margin Notes

Creating margin notes is sometimes easier and more efficient than highlighting. Instead of highlighting, use a pen or pencil and place a vertical line down or a bracket around the margin of a useful paragraph. Immediately reread the paragraph and decide what is most important. Then put a few of your own key words and abbreviations in the margin. For example, if you were to put margin notes next to the same paragraph highlighted above, the margin notes might read: "3 reasons why ineffective highlighting postpones learning." If you had to go back over this material for work or school, you would then either pass over the paragraph because you knew the reasons or you would quickly review it looking for the three reasons. If you highlighted and made margin notes, you would spend more time initially creating the notes but spend less time reviewing.

Taking Full Notes

Taking full notes is time-consuming but very valuable for learning unfamiliar material or documenting details. Write each heading the writer uses for new topics on the left side margin (preferably three inches wide) of your notepaper and then write details on the right side. What you are doing is taking the reading and putting it into your own words in outline form. This works extremely well for nonfiction, factual material.

For fiction, taking full notes means creating a system of keeping track of the characters, plot, conflicts, climaxes, resolutions, and so on. Your system can be as simple as using index cards tucked into the book jacket or as elaborate as creating a notebook for it.

If you are reading for pleasure, even just keeping your own cast of characters and list of events is useful, especially if you find yourself reading only a little over a long period of time. Note taking will reduce your frustration with having to go back to find out who is who and what happened when.

If you are reading for school and you need to know many details, including who said what and what happened when, it is a good idea to read a chapter and then document what you think the most important characters and events are. In effect, you are predicting what the instructor may ask on a test.

Try This with a Newspaper or Magazine

Find something you have to read—perhaps a newspaper or magazine article. Experiment using effective highlighting, margin notes, or full notes. See which method works best for you. Remember to take notes only if your purpose and responsibility require it. Otherwise, you are probably wasting your time.

Start Your Engines:
The Right Side Pull

In Day 1, I described the reasons for and uses of "Adding a Stick Shift to Your Reading." You might want to go back to this section to refresh your memory about pacers. Remember you may find that not all the pacers work for you. However, give each a try and stick with the ones that feel most comfortable.

The Right Side Pull, opposite of the Left Side Pull (see Day 2), is a pacer that helps focus your eyes at the end of the line as well as helps keep your place reading down the text. You may also find that you prefer using the Right Side Pull. Choose a page in a magazine, newspaper, or this book to experiment with. Place your pointed index finger of either hand at the end of the line on the right side of the paragraph. There should be nothing else in your hand. As you read across a line to your finger, slowly but continually move your finger down the right side of the column. As you get more accustomed to this technique, try moving your finger a little faster.

Gauge Your Attitude

Let's take an attitude check. Write down or mentally fill in the blank of the following statement:

I am a(n) _____ reader.

Is your reading attitude changing?

 ## Pit Stop: Tip of the Day

Becoming aware of what distracts you is usually not a one-time event. When you make a change in your reading environment, you may find another distracter that you didn't think about. For example, you decide to move to the company cafeteria during off hours to get some quiet time. You didn't know that another department uses the room for group meetings. You now need to find another location.

Do the best you can to ensure an effective reading environment. But be willing to change where you are and also to accept the fact that you are human. This means you will find times when reading is just not possible.

In Day 4, you will learn about the three speed techniques for your eyes. They will help you widen your eye span, taking in more words at a glance. Comprehension will be challenged, but by using these techniques your brain will catch up. Read on!

Getting Up to Speed

This chapter is going to be a lot of fun. You will have opportunities to play with your eyes and brain. You will experiment with the many ways of increasing your eye span. If you find the method(s) that work best for you and make them part of your reading routine, then you will read more in less time with better comprehension.

As you learn to widen your eye span and take in more at a glance, initially your brain may have some difficulty with comprehension. To best explain this, think of your eyes as the window to your brain. If your eyes right now only take in one word at time, then your brain only processes one word at a time. However, as you begin to open your window (your eye span) wider, initially your brain might be overwhelmed by the amount of information it receives. But by repetitively using the new strategies, your brain will adjust to its new window span and catch on beautifully.

So as you learn about the faster reading tactics, do not become overly concerned with your comprehension—yet. You need to learn to get comfortable with the mechanics of the faster engine before you can take it on the road.

Stopping on Key Words

You may have been taught and continue to believe that you must read every word. Anything less is "cheating." This belief stems from your elementary school teachers who taught you, and rightfully so, that you must read every word. Back then you were learning how to read; you needed to process every word because you were learning what words looked like and what they meant. At that time you didn't have enough experience to make educated guesses about their meaning from contextual clues. If you haven't had any reading training since elementary school, reading every word may still be your practice.

Also, you were left with the impression that if you read every word, you would surely understand its meaning. If you read every word now, does that guarantee comprehension? No. Is it a good use of your time? Definitely not. Thankfully as an adult, you now have a solid foundation of background knowledge of words and their meanings that will enable you to use and benefit from the faster reading strategies.

The method of stopping your eyes on key words is a powerful reading strategy that can immediately increase your reading speed. It also reduces subvocalization. Key words are generally the *bigger*, more important words in a sentence. They are usually longer than three letters in length and carry the meaning of the sentence. For example, most people read the following eleven-word sentence word for word:

The task is defined by a series of steps and elements.

By looking for and stopping your eyes only on the key words, you can still understand the sentence while saving time. Read just the five underlined key words below:

The *task* is *defined* by a *series* of *steps* and *elements*.

Now look at the six words that are *not* underlined. How many times have you seen those in your lifetime? Do you see how the underlined words naturally carry the most meaning of the sentence? Think about what would happen to your reading if you could read, or stop your eyes on, five words out of eleven while still understanding what you read. The result? At least a doubling of your reading speed.

Reading the big, or key, words does *not* mean you are skipping words. What you are doing is focusing your eyes on the longer words while incorporating the others in one glance/eye stop. In effect, you are expanding your eye span. This is why comprehension is possible.

When you start to experiment with this technique, know that there are no right or wrong key words. If you have too many, you will waste your time and you will tend to subvocalize more. If you read too few, you may not understand what you read.

Experiment with Key Words

Take a pen or pencil and quickly underline the bigger words of the paragraph below. Go for length, not meaning. Do not be surprised if you end up underlining every other word or maybe even a few in a row. If your eyes stop on a word and you aren't sure whether it is a key word or not, underline it anyway. Just do it quickly.

> Homeopathy is a system of medicine that is based on the principle that "like cures like." That is, if a substance can cause symptoms in a healthy person, then it can stimulate self-healing of similar symptoms in a sick person. The truth of this principle has been verified experimentally and clinically for the last 200 years. The exact mechanism by which homeopathy works is unknown, but 200 years of clinical experience along with research have confirmed homeopathy's effectiveness.
>
> (Used with permission from the National Center for Homeopathy newsletter, *Homeopathy Today,* Alexandria, Virginia, November 1999.)

When you have finished, reread the paragraph, stopping your eyes only on the words you underlined. See if you need to make any changes that would help you better understand the passage. Know that you may naturally stop your eyes on the first word of a sentence, no matter its length or importance. This is because it is an important starting point for the brain and an eye stop worth keeping.

The sample paragraph about homeopathy contains seventy-eight words, with about forty-five as key words. Count your underlines and see if you are close to this number. As you become more skilled at locating key words, you will notice that you become more proficient at finding not only the longer words but also the ones that have the most meaning. You still may stop your eyes on a word like "if," "and," "but," or "that," but they are not key words. Remember, as long as you are actively seeking out the bigger, more important words, you will read faster while maintaining comprehension.

Now try reading the key words without underlining on either another page in this book or a piece of material from your read later pile. In the beginning, use underlining only to help you become familiar with the technique. You can do it again anytime you want to jump-start your key word reading. However, if you continue to underline, you will reduce your speed and efficiency.

Exercise: Eye Swing

You can train your eyes to pick up key words. Learning to "swing" your eyes helps them become more familiar with the efficient eye movements necessary for faster reading. With a little practice, you develop a smooth reading rhythm.

Begin reading by stopping your eyes on the thick line at the beginning of the first line. Then jump your eyes over the dots to the next thick line. Continue to the end of the paragraph. Do not move your head: Let your eyes do the moving. Try this exercise several times as quickly and as accurately as you can. You can return to this exercise whenever you feel it is necessary.

Exercise: Discipline Your Eyes

This exercise was originally published in 1956 in *Reading Improvement for Adults* by Paul Leedy (McGraw-Hill), and to this day I still use it effectively in my seminars. It is a simple yet incredibly powerful drill for building efficient eye movements.

1. On the inside cover of this book, or on a separate piece of paper, make a date and time chart like this one:

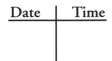

2. Put today's date under the date column.

3. With a clock with a second hand next to you or a stopwatch, time how long it takes to read the exercise. It may take you as long as two minutes or as little as thirty seconds.

- Read across the lines, not down.

- Read for comprehension

The purpose   of this drill   is to discipline

the little muscles   that move the eyes   from left to right.

Incorrect habits   of reading   have frequently caused

these muscles   to behave   in an undisciplined

and inefficient manner.   Try to make   your eyes march ahead

in three   rhythmic leaps   across the line.

Try to feel   the tiny tug   on these six

little muscles   that move each eye.   You will note

that some phrases   are short   others are longer.

This is done   intentionally.   The amount

of line width   that various people   can see differs

with the individual.   In these exercises   try to group

as one eyeful   all the words   in the unit;

look at a point   just about midway   in each word group.

At times   you will feel   as though the field

of your vision   is being stretched.   So much the better!

At other times   the phrase will be   too short.

We shall strive   for wider and wider   units as we proceed.

In that way   your eyes will grasp   more and more

at a glance.   Read this exercise   two or three times

every day   for a few days.   Try always

to cut down   on the time   that it took you

to read it   each preceding time.   You will soon get

the knack of it.   Give it a strong,   fleeting glance.

See it all   in one look;   then be off

to see the next   and the next,   and so on

to the very end   of the exercise.   And now,

how long   did it take you   to read this?

Write your time   on the chart   in this book.

4. Now write your total time in minutes and seconds next to today's date under the time column.

At this point, you have read and understood what the exercise described. You now have something extremely valuable you did not have a minute ago. Can you guess what it is? What is one of the most valuable pieces of information you can have as a reader? Background knowledge! Use this knowledge to really help you push yourself on this exercise.

Now read this exercise again, timing yourself. But this time *read for speed, not comprehension.* Then track your score on your time chart. On your mark, get set, go!

When you read it the second time, you may have felt a reading rhythm of three stops and three jumps across the line. Because your eye muscles were stretched out from the first time you did the exercise, the words flowed better to your eyes the second time. If you can identify the intended rhythm of this exercise, then it is easier to re-create it with your own material.

Your timing goal of the exercise is between fifteen and forty seconds. If you can consistently read this within this time frame, you are well on your way to building efficient eye movements.

Now that you are familiar with both the Eye Swing and Discipline Your Eyes, which works best for you?

Reading Thought Groups

Reading key words is a powerful method for reducing the mental whispering and engaging your brain to actively seek out the more important words in a sentence. Another equally powerful technique is called reading thought groups, also known as phrasing. The Discipline Your Eyes exercise already introduced you to this method.

Take a look at the following paragraph and review the thought groups. They are separated by slash marks.

Phrasing/is reading/a group of words/that form a thought./ By looking for/these thought groups,/you force your eyes/to move forward faster/while maintaining/good comprehension./

The first sentence of the above paragraph has eleven words with four thought groups. The second sentence has eighteen words with six thought groups. Learning to grasp a thought during an eye stop is certainly more efficient than only grasping a word at a time. Your brain will be actively engaged in finding the words that have related meaning.

Experiment with Thought Groups

Take a pen or pencil and quickly find the thought groups in the same paragraph below. Make a slash mark where you think one thought ends and another one begins.

> Homeopathy treats the whole person—physical, mental, emotional—and it treats each person individually. For example, a homeopath treating a cold sufferer does not presume that all colds are alike, but instead asks about the person's unique symptoms such as: Is the person chilly or flushed? Is the nose running or stuffed up? Did the cold come on after stress, anger, or loss of sleep? The homeopath tries to get a complete picture of the person's individual experience of the cold. Then the homeopath chooses a homeopathic medicine that best matches this person's symptom picture.
>
> (Used with permission from the National Center for Homeopathy newsletter, *Homeopathy Today*, Alexandria, Virginia, November 1999.)

When you have finished, review the paragraph, reading your thought units to see if they make sense. The above paragraph has ninety-five words with about thirty thought units. It doesn't matter how small or large your thought group is; just make sure the words form a thought. Imagine what getting into the habit of reading phrases will do for your ability to read faster. It also ensures comprehension because you are reading thoughts, not just one unrelated word at a time.

Now try reading thought groups without slash marking on either another page in this book or a piece of material from your read later pile. In the beginning, use slash marking only to help you become familiar with the technique. You can do it again anytime you want to jump-start your phrase reading.

However, if you continue to use the slash mark, you will reduce your speed and efficiency.

Reading Key Phrases

Some people, like myself, have found that actually combining key words and phrases into a technique I call *key phrases* is quite powerful. There is no right or wrong way to do it and really no specific way to teach it. It is just an active way for the brain to read what is most important, either a key word or phrase, quickly.

You can mix the two methods yourself. It may mean reading one sentence using key words and the next using phrases. It may mean reading a key word, then another key word, then a phrase, then another key word, then a phrase in the same sentence. Experimenting through trial and error will help you figure out what works best for you.

After experimenting with each of these methods, you may intuitively know which one you'd like to keep and use. No matter which you choose, each is an improvement over one word at a time.

Yellow Flag: Caution, Caution, Caution!

There are a few things you need to know about these speed techniques:

- **Using key words naturally reduces the talking.**
  Reading key words naturally helps you reduce mental whispering. However, reading in phrases, not key phrases, can encourage more talking or individual word

reading. So if you are a talker, then key words may be a better method for you.

- **Watch column width.** If the column width of your reading material is wider than a newspaper column, then you can use key words and/or phrasing easily. However, if the column width is about six words per line, such as a newspaper column, you will drive yourself crazy constantly trying to wrap your eyes around to the next line finding the thought groups. Therefore, you may find reading key words more helpful than thought groups on narrow-column material.

- **Learn to push the pedal.** When you start using these faster reading methods, you want to really push yourself to see how fast you can go. You will learn through trial and error what works best for you.

 # Time Trial No. 4

Time trials in car racing are done prior to the actual race. They are primarily a test of speed. It is one car against the clock. They test a car and driver's ability to perform at various speeds and on different track conditions, such as curves or straightaways, or in rainy or dry weather.

Up until now, the time trials you have completed included comprehension questions. But as I have explained, the faster reading techniques in this chapter need to be learned on their own before you can even attempt to gauge your understanding. Hence this exercise only tests your reading speed. You will get a preliminary idea of how efficient or effective you might be using these new tools on your engine.

On the following practice reading, choose either key

words, phrases, or key phrases as described in this chapter. Remember not to use your pen to underline or slash-mark anymore. You can add in a hand or card pacer if you like. While reading, be aware of any distracters like daydreaming, regressing, or mental talking.

1. Using your chosen faster reading method, time yourself for exactly one minute on the following reading. If you finish the text before the minute is up, return to the beginning of the passage and continue until the minute is complete.

2. Mark the line you are on at the end of the minute. Directions continue after the reading.

The History of Speed Reading
By Pam Mullan
1,211 words

People have been concerned with systematically increasing reading speeds since 1925. This is when the very first formal Speed Reading course was conducted at Syracuse University in the United States. But at many times in writing
5   history, literate people have considered how to speed up the reading process. For example, in the mid-1600s, a man named Antonio di Marco Magliabechi was reportedly able to read and comprehend and memorize entire volumes at a rapid rate. But while 1925 appears to be the first formal
10 presentation of a Speed Reading course, much research in the area was being conducted before that date.

It was a French ophthalmologist, Emile Javal, who unknowingly laid the foundations of Speed Reading with his eye-movement experiments in 1878. Javal discovered that
15 the eyes move in a series of jumps (saccades) and pauses (fixations), stopping on average three or four times, while reading a line of text. It is only during these fixations, when the eyes are steady, that word recognition can occur. Prior to Javal's work, it had been believed that the eyes

20 would stop on each letter, or at least each word, while reading.

His discovery was foundational because it demonstrated that our field of focus (number of characters that the eyes can recognize per glance) is wider than previously imag-
25 ined. If our eyes can fixate on a number of words at a time "naturally," then perhaps we are capable of reading faster than commonly believed. It did not take people long to challenge the knowledge of the day and ask how reading rates could be improved upon. As early as 1894, articles
30 were being published in magazines, such as *The Educational Review*, about the advantages and methods of Speed Reading.

Coupled with the increased interest and desire to improve reading speeds was the mass public education of the
35 late 19th and early 20th centuries. At that time, literacy rates were rapidly increasing in the United States, which in turn prompted more people to read—for business, learning, and pleasure. These increases not only generated a great demand for printed materials, but also prompted re-
40 search interest in the area of text legibility.

Legibility, for conventional print, denotes how physical characteristics of written text affect factors such as visual fatigue, reading speed, and comprehension. While publishers were interested in the quality and appearance aspects of
45 printed materials, reading researchers focused on the relationship between physical characteristics of text and its effect on the outcome, visual fatigue, speed, and comprehension. The concept of Speed Reading at that time focused very little on visual or perceptual elements, but focused more on sheer
50 effort on the reader's part in order to improve.

Further advancements in Speed Reading were made by an unlikely group, the United States Air Force. Their discoveries represent the first large-scale usage and acceptance of Speed Reading as a phenomenon, and stemmed from the
55 life-and-death experiences of their pilots. Tacticians noticed that some pilots had difficulty identifying aircraft from long distances. The goal of the tacticians and the United States Air Force was to improve the visual acuity of their pilots.

The psychologists and educational specialists working
60 on the visual acuity question devised what was later to become the icon of early Speed Reading courses, the tachistoscope. The tachistoscope is a machine designed to flash
images at varying rates on a screen. The experiment started
with large pictures of aircraft being displayed for partici-
65 pants. The images were gradually reduced in size and the
flashing rate was increased. They found that, with training,
an average person could identify minute images of different planes when flashed on the screen for only one-five-
hundredth of a second.
70   The results had obvious implications for reading, and
thus began the research into the area of reading improvement, using the tachistoscope. Using the same methodol-
ogy as in the aircraft example, the Air Force soon
discovered that they could flash four words simultaneously
75 on the screen at rates of one-five-hundredth of a second,
with full recognition by the reader.
The training demonstrated clearly that, with some
work, reading speeds could be increased. Not only could
they be increased but the improvements were made by im-
80 proving visual processing. Therefore, the next step was to
train eye movements by means of a variety of pacing techniques in an attempt to improve reading.
The reading courses that followed used the tachistoscope to increase reading speeds, and discovered that read-
85 ers were able to increase their speeds from 200 to 400
words per minute using the machine. The drawback to the
tachistoscope was that post-course timings showed that,
without the machine, speed increases rapidly diminished.
Following the tachistoscope discoveries, Harvard Uni-
90 versity Business School produced the first film-aided
course, designed to widen the reader's field of focus in
order to increase reading speed. Again, the focus was on visual processing as a means of improvement. Using machines to increase people's reading speeds was the trend of
95 the 1940s. While it had been clearly established that reading speed increases of 100% were possible and had been at-
tained, lasting results had yet to be demonstrated.

It was not until the late 1950s that a portable, reliable, and "handy" device would be discovered as a tool to promote
100 reading speed increases. The researcher this time was a mild-mannered school-teacher with a passion for underachievers and reading, named Evelyn Wood. Not only did she revolutionize the area of Speed Reading, but she committed her life to the advancement of reading and learning development.
105   Her revolutionary discovery came about somewhat by accident. She had been committed to understanding why some people were natural speed readers, and was trying to force herself to read very quickly. While brushing off the pages of the book she had thrown down in despair, she dis-
110 covered, quite accidentally, that the sweeping motion of her hand across the page caught the attention of her eyes, and helped them move more smoothly across the page. That was the day she discovered the hand as a pacer, and called it the Wood Method.
115   Not only did Mrs. Wood use her hand-pacing method, but she combined it with all of the other knowledge she had discovered from her research about reading and learning, and she introduced a revolutionary new method of learning, called Reading Dynamics, in 1958.
120   It made its debut in "Speech 21" at the University of Utah. It was so dramatically effective that students and faculty anxiously stood in line for hours waiting for an open desk.
        Mrs. Wood introduced Reading Dynamics to the public in 1959, having piloted the program at the University
125 of Utah for a year. She moved to Washington, D.C., and opened the first Evelyn Wood Reading Dynamics Institute. Soon, her institutes were all over the world. Evelyn Wood's name became synonymous with Speed Reading. She sold the business in 1967, but continued to teach.
130 Mrs. Wood died in 1995 at the age of 86.
        In viewing the various trends of the history of speed reading, it stands out quite clearly that one method used consistently throughout is the training of the eyes to move more effectively. Whether it is a tachistoscope, a film-aided
135 approach, or the hand as a natural pacer, this element remains today to help increase a reader's speed.

(Used with permission from Pamela Mullan, corporate reading consultant.)

3. Now count the number of lines you have just read using the numbers in the margin to guide you. If you went back to the beginning, add those lines onto the total number of lines in the article.

4. Multiply the number of lines you read by 9. 9 is the average number of words per line of this reading.

> Number of lines read _____ x 9 words per line =
> Words per Minute

> *Important note:* You may be uncomfortable with your comprehension. Go to "What, You Don't Understand?" later in this chapter for some reassuring words.

5. Track your Time Trial score: Go to your Personal Progress chart on page 204 and fill in *only* your Words per Minute and the date you did this exercise. Compare your speed scores to the previous readings.

Just when you thought you learned all you needed to know about increasing reading speed, here are two more methods to try.

Fast Tracks: Reading Between the Lines

To help break the overlearned habits of focusing on every or almost every word on a line, you might find it helpful to practice reading between the lines. You do this by stopping not on the line of print itself, but on the white space just above each line. It is possible to read words only by looking at the top half of letters. Try to figure out what each sentence says below. The first one has the top half of the letters covered while the second one has the bottom half covered. Which one is easier to predict?

~~Reading the bottom of words is quite challenging.~~
~~The tops of letters provide shape and form for making predictions~~

You can practice reading between the lines anytime you read. For example, try reading between the lines with the paragraph below.

When you read between the lines, you become aware of a new sensation of freedom from individual words as fixation points. This sensation will be uncomfortable at first but can lead to considerable increases of speed.

Reading between the lines is a technique perfectly suited for your daily reading. You can also use it with key words, phrases, and/or key phrases.

Indenting

The vertical lines you see are here for a purpose. Another technique, which for some students produces immediate speed gains, is to shorten each line at both the left and right. That is, if the last fixation you make on each line falls at the extreme right end, there is nothing but a blank margin for your peripheral vision to take in on the right side. Similarly, if your return sweep carries you all the way to the extreme left of each new line, there is nothing but a blank margin to the left of your first fixation. This prevents you from efficiently using one or both sides of your peripheral vision.

Indenting means simply stopping your eyes on the first line about half an inch inside the left margin and ending it about a half an inch before the right margin. The lines down the sides of these paragraphs show approximately where your first and last fixations should fall. As a result, you can eliminate a total of one full fixation each line.

The first several times you try this technique, you can actually draw similar lines down the sides of the page as reminders to your eyes until you feel comfortable. If you are stopping your eyes seven or eight times a line, by cutting down just one stop per line, you can increase your reading speed by more than 10 percent. Try it!

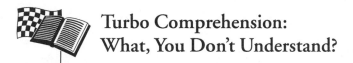

Turbo Comprehension: What, You Don't Understand?

At this point in the faster reading process, you may be feeling uncertain about your comprehension. And rightfully so. Remember the window analogy from the beginning of this chapter? The brain is overwhelmed by all the information you are feeding it.

By using these strategies on your reading in the next few days, you will find that your conscious mind begins to catch on. *Reading faster then becomes a tool to help you get the comprehension you want.*

It is possible that if I had provided comprehension questions for Time Trial No. 4, you could have fared better than you thought. This is because the unconscious mind knows the answers even though the conscious mind isn't aware yet. Good comprehension depends on many factors. If ten people read the same thing, you could easily get varying opinions about its meaning. This is because you read with your own filters based on your background knowledge and experiences.

So comprehension is made up of what is really said and how you interpret what is said. Anyone who has ever been in a book club knows about the heated discussions that ensue as a result of different minds reading the same book.

Some factors that influence good comprehension include:

- Knowing why you are reading and what you are reading for (Day 3).

- Connecting new information to existing knowledge (Day 5).

- Concentrating when you read (Day 3).

- Being willing to receive more information—not preoccupied (Day 3, Day 5).

- Knowing where the author is going before you begin (Day 5).

- Adjusting your reading speed according to your purpose (Day 8).

- Understanding the vocabulary (Day 9).

- Evaluating what was really said first, then interpreting it your own way (Day 6).

- Reading actively (Days 1–10).

On the Road to Building Proficient Skills

This chapter introduces many reading methods, which I call tools. However, these tools are not skills. Skills are built over time by repetitively using tools.

A familiar analogy can be made by comparing reading to golf or tennis. Pretend you are an average golfer or tennis player. If your goal is to improve your game, you must learn the elements of better strokes and practice specific exercises to perfect the skill. Similarly in reading, you must learn the elements of efficient and effective reading and practice specific exercises to master the skill. Initially, you are acutely aware of each new movement you make. You may feel less competent than before and wonder if the new moves really work. But as you persist, the intense awareness and feelings of awkwardness recede, paving the way for increased confidence and competence.

Another Important Word About Your Brain

Your brain is prewired with the neurons needed to learn language. If you watch a child develop from infancy, you witness his or her speech development. Your brain, though innately able to learn language, is not prewired for reading. Reading needs to be taught. You first learn how to decode letters, then words, until the act of reading becomes automatic or procedural. Learning how to read faster is like understanding how to decode words in a more efficient way.

Pat Wolfe, an educational consultant from Mind Matters, Inc., and a specialist in brain research, says that procedural memory is sometimes called muscle memory. She says that if you use a sequence repeatedly, eventually it becomes automatic. Eventually the sequence becomes instinctive as you become more of an expert, leaving the brain with less work to execute the procedure. If you do it enough times, you instruct the brain to begin the sequence, which in turn triggers your body's memory of the procedure. In effect, you program your brain through repetition of movement and activity. Eventually the sequence is automatic, like learning to tie your shoes, driving a stick shift car, playing the piano, or riding a bicycle. *Though the faster reading skills can become automatic, your brain must still be active, conscious, and mindful to trigger them.* So each time you experiment with faster reading strategies, the closer you are to becoming the master of the procedure.

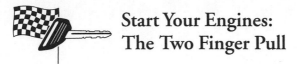

Start Your Engines: The Two Finger Pull

The Two Finger Pull is a pacer that uses the index fingers of both hands. They help focus your eyes primarily on the line you are reading as well as keep your place reading down the lines. Choose a page in a magazine, newspaper, or this book for this exercise. Make sure it is on a flat surface, not balanced upright in your hands. Place the index finger of your left hand at the beginning of the line and the index finger of your right hand at the end of the same line. Your fingers are now framing the line of text. There should be nothing else in your hands. As you read, quickly move your eyes from the left finger to the right and back again, slowly but continually moving your fingers down the left and right side of the column. You can use key words, phrases, or key phrases to help you go faster. As you get more accustomed to the method, try moving your index fingers a little faster.

Gauge Your Attitude

Let's take an attitude check. Write down or mentally fill in the blank of the following statement:

I am a(n) _____ reader.

Is your reading attitude changing?

 ## Pit Stop: Tip of the Day

When starting to use the faster reading methods presented in this chapter, I suggest you experiment only on reading material that is familiar. Remember initially you are going for speed, so you want to make comprehension as easy as possible. In the first few days of learning how to drive a stick shift car, would you like to drive in San Francisco or Boston? Or would you rather drive on the flat, no-traffic, straight plains of the Midwest where there are no great driving challenges and no surprises? In a short time, though, you would be able to navigate the steep San Francisco hills or the famous traffic circles in Boston. Just get used to the mechanics of the car first.

In Day 5, you will learn ways to obtain background knowledge from nonfiction material before reading it. It will also be a priceless tool for weeding through your read later stack.

Reading the Road Map

Have you ever taken a car trip without directions? Imagine setting out to go somewhere you have never been without having the slightest idea of how to get there. How might you feel? Perhaps frustrated because you don't know where you are going, or not confident that you will actually reach your destination, or confused about which way to go. Not a fun trip! Do these questions reflect how you sometimes feel after you start reading?

Unfortunately, this scenario is very close to what unskilled readers do when they read. They approach their reading like a car trip without directions. They find something to read that they know nothing about, jump right in at the first word, and continue reading until the end. They become frustrated because they feel obligated to read the entire thing. Remember, your elementary school teacher left you with the impression that you had to read it all, or else. These readers feel uncertain that they are really understanding what they are supposed to or confused because the reading isn't what they had expected. It is no wonder that many people do not enjoy reading.

One sure way to avoid going into any reading situation completely blind is to first tap into your background knowledge. Remember, your background knowledge consists of the unique things you have personally learned and experienced. Each piece of your background knowledge can be considered a *clue* to a reading's meaning.

Clue In Your Brain!

Race car drivers prefer tracks they have raced before and dislike new ones. This is consistent with human nature—because we like things we are familiar with, or have clues about. We feel more challenged by the unfamiliar when we are clueless. If drivers are unfamiliar with the track layout such as the sharpness of its curves or where the pit lane is located, they cannot mentally prepare nor focus their minds by visualizing how the race may proceed.

Similarly, reading unfamiliar material makes comprehension and focus a challenge. You might feel like you are in the middle of a thick forest without any idea how to get out. Gaining familiarity with the unfamiliar is achieved by looking for clues, any piece of information that will give you a reassuring feeling that you are in the right place. Clues guide you in making decisions and interpretations from what you read. The more clues you have before you start reading, the faster you can read with good comprehension.

So you may be wondering how you get background knowledge on a track you have never seen before? Or how do you know if you have any to begin with? The best way is to get a road map.

Getting the Map Before You Begin

Savvy drivers know that road maps show you the world. A road map tells you where you are, where you have been, and where you are going. It tells you about your surroundings and, sometimes more importantly, what's not around you, like a gas station or rest stop.

Securing a road map before any car trip assures a pleasant journey. A pleasant journey could mean feeling comfortable about where you are going, confident you will make it there in a timely fashion, and positive you are on the right road. Some people like having a map to plot the quickest way from point A to B. Others use a map to plan a leisurely trip by looking for all the scenic country roads. For any reason, knowing before you begin what you want out of the trip and where the journey can take you is extremely efficient.

When taken a "reading trip," the way to locate the road map is to use a strategy called *pre-viewing*. Pre-viewing is a conscious, specific technique of looking over a piece of reading material *before* actually reading it. It is a deliberate skimming process that provides you with the writer's outline so you know the direction of the reading before you begin. As a result you can:

- Decide whether the reading is worth your time.

- Establish a more specific purpose and responsibility.

- Gain valuable background knowledge that helps you read more efficiently and effectively.

Pre-viewing can be applied to any nonfiction reading, including but not limited to newspaper and magazine articles, chapters in instruction manuals and textbooks, reference guides, newsletters, e-zines, and more. This pre-viewing process *cannot* be applied to fiction, since fiction has a different inherent structure.

While pre-viewing's primary purpose is to provide you with background knowledge about material you have not seen before, the process also serves as:

- A replacement for reading everything in detail.

- An introduction to any reading.

- A review process that reduces rereading.

For whichever reason you use it, pre-viewing is a powerful and extremely efficient reading tool.

Pre-viewing dispels the commonly held notion that the only way to read is to start from the beginning and read to the end. Many people believe that just because something is written and printed that they have to read every word.

When you began reading this chapter, did you just start reading all the words from the beginning? Or did you look at anything, like skimming through the subheads, before jumping in?

Reading directly from beginning to end is not always the most effective or efficient way to read any material. Instead, before you read, quickly look for important clues that help you build background knowledge and establish your reading road map.

Do you remember in high school or college when your instructors required you to create an outline before you started writing a rough draft of an essay or paper? Those who graduated into nonfiction writing or editing careers still follow this sage advice. As a result, *there is an outline inherent in all nonfiction reading material.*

Outlines provide the structure and organization of written ideas. Usually they summarize the main points and can be easily located in heads and subheads.

Take a look at the following reading road map legends, in symbol form, and the corresponding reading clue location.

#>>>>§T_T_T_T_§T_T_T_§T_T_T_<< (???)

The Reading Road Map

Road Map Legend	*Reading Clue Location*
#	Name of the trip = Title
>	Where the trip begins = Introduction
Paragraph §	Big cities along the way = Subheads
T	Towns along the way = The first sentence of paragraphs
_	Roadways = Paragraphs
<	Where the trip ends = Summary or concluding paragraphs
(?)	Are you sure you made it? = Questions at the end (textbooks only)

Keep in mind that not all nonfiction has all these clues but most do. Apply only those that correspond to your reading material. Below is an abbreviated version of "The History of Reading" from Day 4 with added subheads to give you an idea how the symbols apply to reading. After you review the passage, review the explanation for each symbol and think about how you activate your background knowledge when you look for this information.

The History of Speed Reading

> I. People have been concerned with systematically increasing reading speeds since 1925. This is when the very first formal Speed Reading course was conducted at Syracuse University in the United States. But at many times in writing history, literate people have considered how to speed up the process. For example, in the mid-1600s, a man named Antonio di Marco Magliabechi was reportedly able to read and comprehend and memorize entire volumes at a rapid rate. But while 1925 appears to be the first formal presentation of a Speed Reading course, much research in the area was being conducted before that date.

§ A. Foundations of Speed Reading

T 1. It was a French ophthalmologist, Emile Javal, who unknowingly laid the foundations of Speed Reading with his eye-movement experiments in 1878. _ _ _

T 2. His discovery was foundational because it demonstrated that our field of focus (number of characters that the eyes can recognize per glance) is wider than previously imagined. _ _ _

T 3. Coupled with the increased interest and desire to improve reading speeds was the mass public education of the late 19th and early 20th centuries. _ _ _

T 4. Legibility, for conventional print, denotes how physical characteristics of written text affect factors such as visual fatigue, reading speed, and comprehension. _ _ _

T 5. Further advancements in Speed Reading were made by an unlikely group, the United States Air Force. _ _ _

§ B. The Advent of the Tachistoscope

T 1. The psychologists and educational specialists working on the visual acuity question devised what was later to become the icon of early Speed Reading courses, the tachistoscope. _ _ _

T 2. The results had obvious implications for reading, and thus began the research into the area of reading improvement, using the tachistoscope. _ _ _

T 3. This training demonstrated clearly that, with some work, reading speeds could be increased. _ _ _

T 4. The reading courses that followed used the tachistoscope to increase reading speeds, and discovered that readers were able to increase their speeds from 200 to 400 words per minute using the machine. _ _ _

T 5. Following the tachistoscope discoveries, Harvard University Business School produced the first film-aided course, designed to widen the reader's field of focus in order to increase reading speed. _ _ _

§ C. Reading Researcher Evelyn Wood

T 1. It was not until the late 1950s that a portable, reliable, and "handy" device would be discovered as a tool to promote reading speed increases. _ _ _

T 2. Her revolutionary discovery came about somewhat by accident. _ _ _

T 3. Not only did Mrs. Wood use her hand-pacing method, but she combined it with all of the other knowledge she had discovered from her research about reading and learning, and she introduced a revolutionary new method of learning, called Reading Dynamics, in 1958. _ _ _

T 4. It made its debut in "Speech 21" at the University of Utah. _ _ _

T 5. Mrs. Wood introduced Reading Dynamics to the public in 1959, having piloted the program at the University of Utah for a year. _ _ _

< II. In viewing the various trends of the history of speed reading, it stands out quite clearly that one method used consistently throughout is the training of the eyes to move more effectively. Whether it is a tachistoscope, a film-aided approach, or the hand as a natural pacer, this element remains today to help increase a reader's speed.

\# **Title:** A nonfiction title gives you a good idea of what the reading will be about. For example:

- Leadership for the Knowledge Era
- Eating Out in Style
- Decorating for the Holidays
- Sibling Rivalry: Just a Myth?

> **Introductory paragraph(s):** If you remember back at
school, every essay had to have a beginning, a middle,
and an end. These parts are commonly known as the
introduction, the body, and conclusion. The first or first
few paragraphs of any article or chapter are the
introduction. They set you up for where your trip is
heading. The introduction may be one paragraph or
several. A rule of thumb is to consider your introduction
over when you read the first subhead, if there is one.

  If you are unsure how much of the introduction to
read, begin by reading the first few paragraphs. If you
are getting the idea of where the reading is going after
the second paragraph, which is very possible, then stop
reading and go to either the first subhead or first
sentence of each paragraph.

§ **Subheads:** Subheads are the big cities on your road
map. They are the backbone of a reading outline and
they give you a strong clue about what might be
discussed. Subheads are often indicated in boldface and
are generally on a line by themselves, often in larger
print than the rest of the text.

T **The first sentence of a paragraph:** The first sentence of
a paragraph gives you the main idea. In school, it was
called a topic sentence. This is probably the most
important clue for knowing what details might be
covered under each subhead. They are like the main
streets of each city your road map takes you through. If
you train yourself to read just the first sentence of every
paragraph, you will be finding an important structure of
the writer's outline.

  Once in a while you may find that the first sentence
is vague or contains an incomplete thought. In that
case, read the second sentence to complete the thought.

__**Roadways:** Roadways are the remaining part of the paragraph not yet read. When you begin using the pre-viewing process, don't read entire paragraphs. Being new to the process, you might be afraid you will miss something and draw yourself back into laborious word-for-word reading. *The idea is to only read those words that will give you the most information in the least amount of time.* It is only after you become comfortable with not reading every word and confident in the pre-viewing process that you can allow yourself to read selected paragraphs in their entirety. The ones you select should be of interest to you as well as only those that meet your reading purpose or responsibility. You are then effectively skimming, not just pre-viewing (see Day 8).

< **Concluding or summary paragraphs (also abstracts):** The end of every piece of writing has a summary or conclusion. It tells you something about the reading. It could be the last line of the reading or the last several paragraphs.

Much research-based writing starts with an abstract, an entire summary of the article, usually just one or two paragraphs. It helps give the reader the background knowledge necessary for understanding the complex concepts presented in the article.

(?) **Questions at the end:** This is meant only for those who are reading textbooks with questions at the end of each chapter. It is effective to review the questions *before* you read the text because they give you your reading responsibility, or what the author intended you to know. Some people think this is cheating. I call it reading actively, fair and square.

When you pre-view a chapter, you can jot down symbols from the road map legend on a separate piece of paper or in the margins of text. For example, you will recognize that the # symbol is the title, the > symbol is the introduction, and the T symbol is the first sentence of the paragraph, and so on.

There are some other places of interest on your road map worth looking at before you begin actual reading. They include:

- Pictures
- Tables
- Graphs
- Charts
- Captions
- Bold print
- Italicized print
- Bulleted points and numbered lists
- Length of reading
- Margin pullouts (pull quotes)
- Separate articles within, sometimes called sidebars or boxes
- Unfamiliar vocabulary
- Author's information
- Copyright date
- Footnotes

- **Pictures, tables, graphs, charts.** By looking at pictures, tables, graphs, and charts you will be able to:
  1. Get a quick visual clue about what the text is discussing.
  2. Increase your reading speed. Have you ever heard that a picture is worth a thousand words?

- **Captions.** Captions usually describe an illustration or photo. They are usually located underneath or directly beside the visual and are helpful in clarifying the image's meaning and text.

- **Bold and italicized print.** Try to become accustomed to using your eyes and brain to find these different type styles. Bold and italicized print tells you:
  1. When a word or words are important to the text's meaning.
  2. When a new vocabulary word is introduced.

- **Bulleted points and numbered lists.** If you were previewing this chapter and quickly read the bulleted points listed before this section, you might have thought, "Okay, I understand. I don't need to read the detailed descriptions below." Or you might have thought, "Okay, I'd like to know why these are so important. I will read the descriptions, or selected ones, below in more detail." Bulleted points and numbered lists do the following:
  1. Communicate a lot of information in a short amount of space.
  2. Help you choose what you need to read in more detail.

- **Length of reading.** By knowing the reading's length before you begin, you can decide:
  1. How you want to manage your time by predicting how long it will actually take you.
  2. Whether the reading topic is worth that much time.
  3. If you want to save it for when you have more time.
  4. How you might break a longer reading down into smaller, more manageable sections.

- **Margin pullouts (pull quotes).** This is a term used for anything printed outside the text in the margin. For example, a margin pullout may give you the following:
  1. Quotes pulled from the reading.
  2. An explanation of a vocabulary term.

- **Separate articles within.** Also known as sidebars or boxes, these can be pre-viewed by looking at the subheadings and first sentences of paragraphs.

- **Unfamiliar vocabulary.** Identifying unfamiliar vocabulary can:
  1. Help you gain a better understanding of the content before you read for detail.
  2. Focus your reading purpose to help you decide whether you need to define the term before you begin to try to figure it out from the context.
  3. Create your own vocabulary list with definitions before you read.

- **Author's information.** Knowing the author's information before you begin reading can:
  1. Give you clues about the author's point of view.
  2. Tell you what experiences have led the author to his or her writing on a particular subject.

- **Copyright date.** The copyright date gives you the following:
  1. When was the writing written? A computer manual from 1993 is probably not up-to-date.
  2. A time context to date the information, indicative of the point of view. You can find the copyright in books near or adjacent to the title page next to the copyright symbol ©.

- **Footnotes.** Footnotes or references are usually found only in academic or research-based writing. Footnotes do the following:
  1. Inform you where the material originated.
  2. Provide more explanation about a specific topic being discussed in the text.

By quickly looking for these clues, you can get the gist of most nonfiction material in a short time. When you add a faster reading strategy to pre-viewing, such as key words, phrases, key phrases, or a pacer, you have a supercharged way of getting the most background knowledge in the least amount of time.

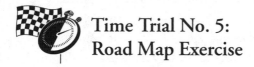 **Time Trial No. 5: Road Map Exercise**

This exercise will take you less than eight minutes. You will be pre-viewing "Day 6: Hanging Out the Caution Flag" for this exercise. You will hopefully find that you will get the gist without reading it in detail. Please read the directions below before turning to Day 6.

1. With a stopwatch or clock with a second hand next to you, get ready to time yourself for five minutes.

2. Begin your pre-view by quickly reading the chapter title, then the introduction, which is the first or first few paragraphs. Remember to use your faster reading strategies to assist you. When you feel you have read enough of the introduction, stop reading in detail.

3. Continue reading just the first sentence of the next and subsequent paragraphs.

4. As you're quickly driving along the writer's road, notice other clues such as illustrations, bulleted points, or bold or italicized print.

5. As you read, be aware your purpose is to piece together the outline until the five minutes are up. If you finish before the five minutes are up, round your time to the nearest 10-second mark. For example, 3 minutes 17 seconds would be 3 minutes 20 seconds.

6. At the end of five minutes, stop your pre-view. *Do not be concerned if you did not get to the end.*

Comprehension Statements

Without looking back at the chapter, respond to the following statements by indicating whether the statement is True (T), False (F), or Not Discussed (N). Take guesses if you are not sure.

_____ 1. A mindful reader is skeptical.

_____ 2. True critical readers only look for the negative things or things they don't like when reading.

_____ 3. There are five main categories of questions you can mentally ask while reading.

_____ 4. The author engages in critical dialogue in this chapter.

_____ 5. Critical people make better critical readers.

_____ 6. There are more facts than opinions in this world.

_____ 7. When an author develops his writing, he may use other words to support his argument.

_____ 8. A word can have different meanings depending on how it is used.

_____ 9. Reading word for word guarantees you will not miss all the small important words.

_____ 10. Critical readers are fast readers.

Now, estimate how many answers you think you have right out of ten _____.

7. Get your words per minute by taking your pre-view time and locating your pre-view Words per Minute on page 207. Then write your pre-view words per minute on your Personal Progress chart on page 205. Realize you did not read every word, which contributes to a faster result. If you compare your scores from previous practice readings, you may be pleasantly surprised by how much faster you read with little or no loss of comprehension. When you learn to pre-view, you spend your time looking for the more meaningful material in the reading.

8. Check your answers on page 201. Document your comprehension percentage on your Personal Progress chart on page 205.

9. Now think about your answers to the following questions:

   • Did you understand more than you thought?

   • How many pages did you get through?

   • Were you able to follow the writer's outline?

   • Were you tempted to read every word? If so, what happened?

   • Did you feel more actively involved in the reading process?

   • Would you go back and read it in more detail now or do you feel you got enough information at this point?

- If you did go back and read it in more detail, how might your reading strategy differ? Would it be faster? Would you have better comprehension?

It's likely that this pre-view test drive was not comfortable for you. It's like you're putting a whole new swing into your golf or your tennis game. It may feel mechanical and shaky at first. You may be concerned about your comprehension. In the beginning, this is more of an exercise in eye movement than comprehension. If your eyes can locate and read just the key information, then comprehension will occur.

Experiment with pre-viewing on all nonfiction reading material in your reading pile. Remember that pre-viewing can serve not only as a replacement for reading in detail, it can also be an introduction or a review. In a short period of time, by experimenting with this pre-view process, you will find it gets easier and more efficient. You may wonder how you ever read without it.

 ## Fast Tracks: The 40/60 Line

What you find in the pre-view road map is what I consider to be the meat of all nonfiction reading material. These clues give you about 40 percent of the key information. The remaining 60 percent is filler, fluff, or explanation. This means you can choose what portion of the remaining 60 percent to spend your time on. You may only need another 20 percent (40 percent pre-view + 20 percent actual reading = 60 percent), which then means you have saved yourself 40 percent of your reading time. You also read actively and got what you needed in less time.

There is no exact order in which to pre-view the clues. It makes sense, however, to chronologically follow the subheads and first sentences of paragraphs to better understand the author's thought process. Let the pre-view clues cue your brain in to what is most important in the reading and, even more importantly, to learn what is of most value to you. Remember that mindfulness is the search for what's meaningful to you. In pre-viewing, this choosing encourages mindfulness and makes you feel more responsible for your outcome. This is a quality of active, mindful readers.

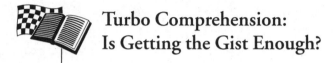

Turbo Comprehension: Is Getting the Gist Enough?

From the pre-view exercise, you might feel you only got the gist of the chapter. And rightfully so. Your purpose for doing the exercise was to try to locate the pre-view clues. Your responsibility was to do it for three minutes and then answer the ten statements to the best of your ability. You were not asked to recite the chapter in detail or to remember it for a test next week. You might, however, be able to talk in general about the chapter's contents.

For much of the reading you have piled up, getting the gist will have to be enough. You do not have time to get more, unless your purpose or responsibility dictates doing so.

Try Using the 5W's and H

If following the pre-view outline seems restricting, remember that you need to adapt it and make it work for you. If you believe that the concept of getting background knowledge is a valuable one, then find the best way for you to get it, given the information in these pages.

An additional way to ensure comprehension is to pre-view or read looking for the 5W's and H: who, what, when, where, why, and how. You can get the key information by looking for the answers to each one of these questions.

Spend Time to Save Time

Many people initially believe that pre-viewing requires a lot of time. Explaining it takes time but doing it is very quick. As you become more skilled, you can pre-view a two-page article in less than a minute or a ten-page chapter in less than five minutes depending on your background knowledge and purpose.

Why take the time to pre-view? Let's take a thirty-minute time frame. Say you have a ten-page chapter that would normally take you thirty minutes to read from beginning to end. Now let's say you pre-view the chapter instead, which takes you eight minutes, leaving you twenty-two minutes to read the chapter in detail. With the background knowledge you found in the eight minutes, you should easily be able to read faster to meet the twenty-two-minute time frame. You actually are likely to read it in less time than that because you found during your pre-view some sections you decided you didn't need to pay much attention to.

Scenario 1	*Scenario 2*
30 minutes to read from beginning to end	8 minutes to pre-view + <u>22 minutes to read detail</u> = 30 minutes

Which thirty minutes is a better use of your time? Which encourages more active reading and better comprehension, after which might you better remember new information?

Which might save you time? The answer to all these questions is Scenario 2. Remember the value of background knowledge; it is great for comprehension but also for speed. A tried and true time management principle applies here: *It takes time to save time.*

Students can also use the pre-view process to *review* before an exam. This saves time by avoiding mindless rereading and focusing on unfamiliar areas.

Newspapers Vary the Road Map

In general, newspaper articles follow a version of the pre-view outline. However, newspaper journalists generally write in an A-frame or inverted pyramid style. They place the most important information at the beginning and slowly work down into less important details of the event or issue covered. This is because if there is a late-breaking story or more advertising, editors cut the story from the end, still keeping the most important details up front. So by reading more detail in the beginning, you get the meat of the story.

Many newspaper articles contain one-sentence paragraphs. This makes reading just the first sentences of paragraphs challenging. You might try reading just the first line, not the complete sentence, of the paragraph to see if you want or need to read more.

Is There Always a Map?

Over the years, I have become an expert pre-viewer. I have also looked at most of the nonfiction material participants bring to my workshops from their reading piles. From this, I would venture to say that about 98 percent of the material followed an understandable pre-view outline.

If you primarily read material that has not gone through an editing process, then you will probably be hard-pressed to find an outline. However, anything that has been published in magazines, e-zines, newspapers, regulation handbooks, computer manuals, and textbooks will all have the pre-view outline.

If you write any material for school or work, you can improve your writing's readability by pre-viewing your own work. See if your main ideas are in the first sentence of your paragraphs. If not, you may have buried them inside the paragraph or not even mentioned them at all. After pre-viewing your own writing, you may wish to edit your work.

Gauge Your Attitude

Let's take an attitude check. Write down or mentally fill in the blank of the following statement:

I am a(n) _____ reader.

Is your reading attitude changing?

Start Your Engines: Pull Down Center

The pacer Pull Down Center works best on narrower-columned material. Choose a page in a magazine, newspaper, or material from your read later pile that's printed in two or more columns per page. Make sure to place it on a flat surface, not balanced upright in your hands. Pick either your right or left index finger and place it in the center of the paragraph under the first line of text. Start reading on the line above your finger. Pull your index finger down the page like a window shade. Pull it as slowly or as quickly as your eyes read each line from side to side. Try stopping your eyes only two to three times per line, seeing more at a glance. Remember to use key words, phrases, or key phrases to help you speed up. As you get more accustomed to the method, try moving it a little faster.

 ## Pit Stop: Tip of the Day

It is no secret that your ability to efficiently read and learn is easier when you are well rested, relaxed, and feeling well. By taking care of yourself and your body's basic needs, you will find the information in this book even more effective. Here are a few health reminders:

- **Find a way to get enough sleep.** Research says the average adult needs between eight and nine hours of sleep a night. If you routinely get under seven hours, you may be compromising your ability to read and learn.

- **Add movement into your day.** By moving, you circulate and oxygenate the blood, making your brain more alert and ready to receive information. Use the stairs instead of the elevator or escalator, park your car farthest from the store's entrance, or if you have a dog walk it at least twice a day. If you have always wanted to get into an exercise routine, here's another justification for doing so. If you use an exercise bike, prop reading material on a stand and read while you move.

- **Eat brain food.** If you are reading to learn and remember, eat foods rich with protein such as cheese or chicken. You can also add vegetables or salad. Avoid sleepy foods such as breads, pretzels, and pasta.

- **Reduce stress.** Though some stress is good, too many experience more stress than is healthy. It is hard to read with good comprehension when you and your body are feeling overwhelmed. You may find some relief by prioritizing what's important to you. To combat the stress bug: Get plenty of sleep, learn deep breathing exercises, and take time to appreciate what you have, not what you wish you had.

Get to know your own personal sleep requirements, exercise needs, food reactions, and stress levels. Only you can set your reading machine up for success.

You are now halfway through your ten-day trial. Day 6 focuses on an important flag—the caution flag. There are many ways to interpret what is read, and Day 6 clarifies how to read with caution.

Hanging Out the Caution Flag

When race car drivers drive, they focus on where they are going and how they are going to get there as quickly and safely as possible. This means they are aware of their surroundings, not what's happening on the other side of the track. The flagman is similar to the driver's eyes on the other side of the track. He waves a yellow caution flag telling the driver to slow down because there is an accident, oil, or other debris on the track. Slowly the driver circles the track waiting for a flag to tell him it's okay to continue. This is a valuable opportunity for drivers to evaluate how the race is going, rethink their racing strategy, and make any adjustments to their driving when the race starts again.

When reading, you not only need to be aware of where you are going but also of what's happening on the author's side. Effective reading is an exchange of ideas, not a one-way conversation. You are the one who converts your reading relationship from a monologue, where you are the passive recipient of the author's words, to a dialogue, where you actively ask questions and look for answers. This is considered critical reading.

A mindful, active reader—one who engages in this dialogue—is also categorized as alert, appropriately suspicious, and skeptical. Though you can think this way while reading fiction, critical reading is primarily meant for nonfiction or information reading.

The Mindful Side of Criticism

If your boss said he wants to speak to you and give you criticism about your job performance, you would probably wonder what you did wrong. However, the word "criticize" means "to consider the *merits and demerits* of and judge accordingly." Ideally, this means that your boss would talk to you about your strengths *and* weaknesses.

Being critical means consciously passing judgment, both favorable and unfavorable, on everything you see, hear, and read. This sometimes is done unconsciously. For example, you go to a new friend's house for dinner. The minute you walk up to the door, your critical mind is working overtime. You are unconsciously evaluating everything you experience from the sound of the doorbell to how the meal tastes to the cleanliness of the bathroom. All of your experiences contribute to your final conscious opinion at the end of the evening.

When you read, your mind works with the same unconscious procedure. If you can learn to criticize consciously and mindfully, however, you will greatly improve your background knowledge and comprehension. How do you accomplish this? By being prepared to look for the pros and cons in what you read, according to you, examine and question carefully, and form your own judgments on the content. Exercising this ability separates the excellent readers from the average ones.

Restaurant critics sample foods and write about what they

like and don't like and why. Movie critics watch movies and use similar criteria. Both share their opinions with their readers based on their background knowledge. Does it mean their criticism is correct? No, there really is no correct criticism just as there is no assurance that you are right in your evaluation of an author's words. Only *you* determine if your evaluation is correct. You base your evaluation on your own background knowledge just as restaurant and movie critics do.

When reading nonfiction, you ultimately want to:

- Justify what you already know is accurate.
- Learn something new.
- Distinguish facts from fiction.
- Change your mind if you are proven wrong.
- Have the author reach a conclusion.

Critical reading, then, is founded on your previous understanding of the subject matter and your current understanding of material you are reading.

There are several ways to create a conscious, mindful relationship with an author when you read. They include challenging the author, distinguishing facts, and making inferences.

Challenging the Author

There are occasions when you read that you are surprised or confused about something an author says. Perhaps the author has not developed a sound argument or her reasoning seems flawed. These are times to use critical and mindful questioning. You may already do this but doing it mindfully makes your reading more active and engaging.

Critical questioning implies that you have a healthy skepticism about the author's motives for the writing and its contents. It is helpful to decide for yourself whether you agree with an author, and, if you disagree, what your basis is for the criticism. The following list of questions, split into three main categories, are valuable when engaging in a hypothetical dialogue between you and an author.

Questions About the Author

Let's look at questions directed toward the author.

- Does the author have experience on this topic?
- Is the writer male or female? Does the gender affect the point of view?
- How does the author's background and experience affect his or her interpretation of the topic?
- What is the author's motive?
- Is the author objective, not influenced by emotions or personal prejudices—or subjective, that is, personal?

Questions About Content

Let's examine queries about content.

- Who is the intended audience for this writing?
- What is the author *literally* saying in the text?
- What is the author really trying to say, or what is he implying? What does he mean?
- Is the message clear?
- Are the details factual or anecdotal?
- Are the arguments and conclusions consistent?

Questions About Yourself

Now think about you and your background knowledge.

- Am I familiar with this author's work? If so, how does this previous experience influence me?
- What do I believe about the piece of reading material?
- Does the information match what I know about the topic? What is different?
- How does this affect what I need to know or what I can use it for?

Ultimately most writers intend to influence your thoughts in some way. If they believe in something, they also want you to believe it. The most objective scientific report, for example, tries to present all the data necessary for you to judge the accuracy of the report's premise or hypothesis. Then the author hopes that you accept his conclusion based upon the data reported.

Use This Book

For example, if you take this book and have a mental dialogue with me, my goal is that you understand the following information based upon the content I have provided in the book and how it is arranged to reach these conclusions. Let's take a look at how I respond to the questions from the three categories above.

Responses from the Author

Keep in mind that my responses are solely my opinion and point of view.

- Some of my experiences are stated on the "About the Author" page as well as related in personal stories throughout the book.

- I am female, although I don't think my gender greatly affects my point of view on this topic.

- My background and experiences learning about and teaching faster reading permit me to be confident about the veracity and usefulness of information in this book.

- My motive for writing this book is to share how simple it is to feel more confident and competent while reading.

- I am definitely influenced by my personal experiences as a reader and an educator. I hope to convert many nonreaders into avid readers.

Responses from the Author About Content

See if you agree with my responses regarding the content presented in this book.

- The intended audience for this book is anyone who wants to feel better about him- or herself as a reader and wants to learn how to read more efficiently.

- Literally, I am saying that if you first become aware of who you are as a reader, and then learn about the many ways you can develop your skills, you can read faster and improve your comprehension.

- I am really trying to say that there is no one preferred way to read more quickly but many possible ways.

- The only way to know which strategies work for you is to try each one and then decide.

- The details are mostly anecdotal, sprinkled with relevant facts.

- I have tried to make my points relevant, clear, and consistent.

Responses from You

Now add in information about yourself and your background knowledge.

- What do you want to believe?

- Does the information match what you know based on your background and experience? What's different?

- Are you getting what you needed to know?

- How can you use it?

Remember, the purpose of asking and then answering these questions is a form of self-dialogue that helps you become an active, mindful, and effective reader.

How to Quickly Prepare for a Business Meeting

Picture this: Your boss tells you that the forty-five-page report you received two weeks ago is going to be the focus of a meeting in twenty minutes. You knew about the meeting but didn't know this report would be discussed. You haven't even looked at it. What do you do? Here are a few suggestions to help you apply your speed reading skills in a time crunch.

- **Pre-view.** Sometimes, you may only have enough time to pre-view. But remember you can get at least 40 to 50 percent of the main points using this strategy. The remaining 50 to 60 percent of the document is usually explanation and elaboration. Look for the writer's outline, if there is one, and, of course, make sure to get the most salient points by reading the introduction, first sentences of paragraphs, and conclusion, and by reviewing any graphics.

- **Look for key words and key phrases.** If time allows you to read in more detail after your pre-view, then put key words, phrases, or key phrases into play. Using your fingers or the white card pacer (remember: top down) will force you out of the tendency to read word for word and help speed your work.

- **Think critically.** First, understand what the author really said and the conclusions the author came up with. Get the facts by looking for the answers to the 5W's and H (who, what, when, where, why, and how). Second, quickly come to your own conclusions based on what you know about the subject and how it relates to the purpose of the meeting.

Many of my workshop participants have told me they have used these strategies and have looked really good in their employer's eyes.

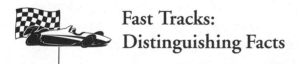 ## Fast Tracks: Distinguishing Facts

A true dialogue is not one-sided: Just as you have the right to question the writer's motives, the author has the right to have you question your own motives and examine your own unacknowledged preconceptions.

Many people have a hard time identifying facts. In my

classes, I do an exercise where I give the participants the definition of the word "fact." Then I ask them to come up with as many facts as they can about a toy, one of the props I use while teaching my class. From about twenty-five responses, maybe only two or three end up being true facts. The remaining responses are opinions, inferences, or biases.

It is a fact that there aren't nearly as many facts as there are opinions in this world. So when in doubt, it is probably an opinion. It is a natural human tendency to be emotionally committed to your own view because it's yours. A strong reaction to an author's statement, either positive or negative, is a clear sign that a bias or a subjective point of view may be at the root of it. Being aware of your opinions, inferences (see below), and biases represents a comprehension challenge every time you read.

Making Inferences

Though you may have heard this already, it is worth repeating: Do not believe everything you read! Just because it's in print doesn't mean it's true. Whenever the media run articles on myself or my business, I am thrilled for the exposure but dread the one inevitable misquote or other inconsistency a journalist may write as a result of our interview. A well-meaning newspaper reporter tried to quote one of the participants in one of my classes. I have changed the participant's name but the quote is accurate.

> "I read word for word very slowly. I'd read a sentence two, three, even four times. My comprehension was terrible," says Ford.
> That was four weeks ago. Now Ford reads at 260 words per minute and her comprehension level is 80 percent.

The reader infers that the progress was good but unfortunately the words per minute and comprehension level quoted was the participant's beginning benchmark instead of her ending average of 580 words per minute with 85 percent comprehension. A big difference.

Two or more people can read the same piece of material and each will have a different interpretation of its meaning. This is the true difficulty of gauging accurate comprehension. People make *inferences* or settle on what they think are logical conclusions based on what they assume is true, given their own background and experiences.

The most intelligent action you can take as a reader is to first read the material and, before inferring its meaning, ask yourself, "What did the author *really* say here?" Avoid jumping to immediate conclusions. Take a mental step back, look for the stated facts, then make your inference based on the evidence presented.

Reviewing Your Notes

Students, business professionals, politicians, and teachers are some of the people who may need to quickly review a set of notes they have made before a meeting, class, or presentation. If you know beforehand that you will want to do a speed review of your notes prior to a presentation or test, for example, you can better prepare your notes for easy review. Here's a two-step process that can make the task easier.

First, go back to "Focus with a Pen in Hand" (Day 3) and review the three useful note-taking strategies: effectively highlighting key words, creating margin notes, taking full notes. By using any or all of these, your notes will be easy and fast to review.

Second, use various pen colors while making notes. Any

color pen will work. For example, use colored pens to show idea transitions or highlight key words. Use different colors to draw quick pictures or graphics to represent the ideas you want to remember. When you review your notes, your eyes will be drawn to the colors and your brain will remember the information better.

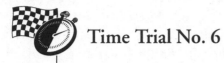 **Time Trial No. 6**

It's time to test your engine. It should take you five minutes or less. On the following practice reading, experiment with some of the information you have learned about. Try using key words, phrases, key phrases, or a pacer. Ensure an appropriate environment for uninterrupted successful reading.

1. **Pre-view the reading first.** Time yourself for a maximum of only thirty seconds, allowing yourself to quickly look at the introduction, the first sentences of the paragraphs, and the questions you will be answering.

2. **Time yourself.** Now see how long it takes to read the passage "It's All Relative" below. Write your total time in minutes and seconds in the space provided at the end of the reading.

It's All Relative

By John D. Whitman

In one sense, the twentieth century really began in 1879 in the town of Ulm, Germany. That year witnessed the birth of Albert Einstein, whose work would overturn the world of physics.

By 1886, Einstein's family had moved to Munich, Germany, and Einstein continued his education there. When his family moved to Milan, Italy, in 1894, Einstein elected to remain behind. He tried to enter a school for electrical engineering in Zurich, Switzerland, but failed the entrance examination. Undaunted, Einstein entered a secondary school, where in 1900 he received a teaching degree in mathematics and physics.

He tried once again to enter a university, but again he was rejected. With the help of a friend, he obtained a job as a patent clerk in Bern, Switzerland. In that patent office, working in his spare time without close contact to any of the other great minds in physics, Einstein changed the world.

By 1905, Einstein had written three papers. Of these, the second was in many ways the most famous. It became known as the Theory of Relativity.

With this paper, Einstein tackled an idea that had nagged at him for years. It had already been proven that light always travels at the same speed. But what happens, Einstein asked, if we chase after a ray of light while we are traveling at the speed of light? We might guess that the light we're chasing would seem to stand still, or at least move more slowly, since we're going at the same rate. But Einstein proved that this was incorrect. Even if you could go that fast, light always seems to be moving away from you at the speed of light. This notion broke every rule of physics known at the time.

This discovery confirmed that many of the laws of physics aren't set in stone. Instead, Einstein's discovery seemed to point to the fact that laws give different results depending on where the observer is standing or how fast he is moving. In other words, results are only meaningful relative to your position in space and time. Nothing is fixed. It's all relative. Einstein submitted his paper to the journal *Annals of Physics,* which was edited by Max Planck, one of the men whose work Einstein had used to create his own theory. Reading through the document, Planck realized that, quietly and calmly, Einstein had turned the scientific world on its head.

Mark your reading time here: _____ (minutes)
_____ (seconds).

3. **Respond to statements.** Immediately answer the
following statements to the best of your ability
WITHOUT looking back at the reading. Estimate the
number of answers you believe are correct and put the
number in the blank provided.

Comprehension Statements

Without looking back at the reading passage, respond to
the following statements by indicating whether the statement
is True (T), False (F), or Not Discussed (N).

_____ 1. Albert Einstein is best remembered for his
work with physics.

_____ 2. Einstein was born in Germany.

_____ 3. Einstein was able to get into any school he
wanted.

_____ 4. Einstein received a degree in teaching.

_____ 5. When Einstein worked in the patent office, he
learned a lot from other scientists.

_____ 6. Einstein married three times.

_____ 7. Einstein's most famous work is his Theory of
Relativity paper.

_____ 8. Einstein set many laws of physics into stone.

_____ 9. Einstein's theory of comparativity states that a
body in motion perceives light differently
than a body at rest.

_____ 10. Max Planck was a close relative of Albert
Einstein.

Now, estimate how many of these answers you believe you
have correct out of ten _____.

4. **Check your responses.** Turn to the Answer Key on page 201. If you have any incorrect, mark the correct response and return to the reading passage to try to understand where you had a problem.

5. **Figure your comprehension percentage.** Add the total number of correct responses you have and multiply by 10. Write your comprehension percentage in your Personal Progress chart on page 205.

6. **Figure your Words per Minute.** Look at your reading time and round off the seconds to the nearest 10-second mark. Turn to the Words per Minute chart on page 207 and find your Words per Minute next to your reading time. Write your Words per Minute in your Personal Progress chart.

7. **Track your Time Trial scores.** Go to your Personal Progress chart on page 205 and make sure you've recorded your Words per Minute, comprehension percentage, and the date you did the exercise. It's also helpful to document other details such as time of day, any preoccupations, strategies used, and so on.

How to Read Challenging Newspaper Articles

Many slow or bored readers tend to skip over the more challenging newspaper articles such as op-ed pieces, letters to the editor, or lengthy features that are newsworthy or of interest but not as pressing as the front-page news. Readers sometimes need more time for these pieces either because of length or the readers may lack background knowledge about the topic. One example is the *New York Times Sunday Magazine*, which typically does not include subheads or natural breaks in its lengthy articles.

Op-ed Pieces and Letters to the Editor

Op-ed (opinion-editorials) pieces are written by newspaper columnists or specialists in a particular field. They present a point of view on a subject generally meant to persuade the reader to think about their position on an issue. Letters to the editor are written by the general public. You can try to preview both types of articles but you may find it challenging. Many times they are written in the first person (using "I"), making it less reportorial and more in the style of a personal opinion. The writing styles vary and are not edited the same way features or breaking-news stories are.

Read the first few lines to get a feel for the writer's position, then skim your eyes down the text looking for content-related key words. Use the speed techniques of key words, phrases, key phrases, or pacers to speed your eyes down the text. Try to gauge the author's emotions and what his point of view is. For example, letters to the editor about charter schools will probably have a certain perspective depending on whether the letter writer is a school principal or a parent.

Lengthy Articles

Lengthy newspaper articles may appear intimidating, especially if you just want to get the meat of the story. Unless you are making a presentation or writing a report about what you read, however, you can get away with not reading the whole article word for word. Reading the introduction, the first sentence of each paragraph, and the conclusion provides you with significant content without all the description and filler information. Then select which paragraphs you want to read in their entirety and which paragraphs you want to skip altogether. Remember to use key words, phrases, key phrases, and pacers to move your eyes along.

Reading Articles Full of Jargon

I would venture to guess that if you own a computer, you have bought and attempted to read a computer magazine. After all, you want to understand how the computer works and how to maximize its use. You may have discovered that computer magazine writers typically do not write for the novice user but rather the information technology specialist or computer expert. No matter how hard you try, your comprehension of the articles is limited because of all the jargon, especially acronyms like HTML and JPEG.

A similar situation arises in the health field. Although there is much health information in magazines, journals, and on the Web, interested or curious nonmedical professionals have a hard time understanding the text. What is a reader to do? Go to medical school?

First, understand that you are not unintelligent, rather, you just lack the necessary background knowledge. You can't be an expert in everything. Fortunately, one great way to get background knowledge (without going to school) is to be persistent and trudge through material, knowing you may only understand 10 to 20 percent. You will probably find the repetition of ideas and concepts over time increases your comprehension. If you see an idea or theory discussed enough in different contexts, it may start to click. If you are not comfortable with only 10 to 20 percent comprehension, then try these strategies:

1. **Pre-view.** I'll say it once again—pre-view! This is a great way to gain preliminary background knowledge. Once you have background knowledge, then you can read in more detail with greater understanding.

2. **Look at different sources.** If you go to *The New England Journal of Medicine* to read about a diabetes

study without much medical or content knowledge, you will not learn a lot or enjoy your reading. Instead, locate material on diabetes that is written for the general public, by the American Diabetes Association, for instance. After a while, you can graduate to those more challenging trade journals in the topic area you're interested in.

3. **Keep a jargon notebook.** If you really want to become well versed in a particular subject, then keeping track of the jargon will give you a personal dictionary for study, review, and reference. In the notebook, write down acronyms and new words on the left margin of your paper. Then try to determine their meaning (either from the content or a dictionary) and write it next to the term. (Acronyms and jargon are usually defined the first time they are used in a reader-friendly article.)

4. **Use speed techniques.** Once you find information on your level, use your speed techniques to quickly help you get what you want without wasting valuable time.

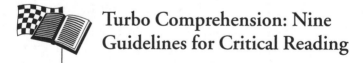 ## Turbo Comprehension: Nine Guidelines for Critical Reading

From the nine guidelines below, choose several or all of them you want to remember and write them down. Tape the paper on a desktop where you read or post it on a wall nearby. By reminding yourself of these guidelines, you increase your comprehension and understanding of the author's message while becoming a more critical reader.

1. Be open-minded about new ideas.

2. Don't argue about things you know nothing about.

3. Know when you need more information.
4. Be aware that people have different ideas about the meanings of words.
5. Know the difference between something that must be true and something that might be true.
6. Avoid hasty generalizations.
7. Question anything that doesn't make sense.
8. Separate emotional and logical thinking.
9. Develop your vocabulary in order to understand others and to make yourself understood.

(From *Critical Thinking Book 1*, by Anita Harnadeck, Midwest Publications Co., Pacific Grove, California, 1976. Adapted by Louise Loomis, director of the Critical Thinking Center for Creativity and Problem-Solving, Hartford, Connecticut. Used with permission.)

Critical Thinking: Engage the Author

Throughout this chapter, I have discussed several ways to hone your critical reading skills. Another way to become a more critical reader or increase your knowledge base is to correspond with an author. For example, let's say an article strikes your interest. By the end of the article, you either like or dislike the author's point of view. Since you are already having a mental conversation with the author concerning your likes and dislikes and/or questioning her point of view, why not engage her in person? I'm not saying to actually meet her, though sometimes it may be possible, but rather to get in touch with her via e-mail or letter.

As an author, I enjoy receiving communications from people who have read my articles or books. The communications range from kudos to negative criticism, and often there are questions about information I have included. This feedback helps me know more about my audience. Usually, I correspond with an individual once depending on the inquiry, sometimes more. Keep in mind that while not all authors will be as receptive, most do write back to their readers to share their expertise, raise their profile, or generate public interest in their field.

As a reader, I have corresponded with authors on several occasions when I have found an author's work stimulating and interesting. From their responses, I have learned more about their work and have found more resources in the same content area. In turn, this has increased my background knowledge. This process enables me to read an author's work critically and with increased comprehension.

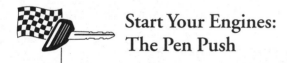 ## Start Your Engines: The Pen Push

There are two ways to perform the pacer known as the Pen Push. Choose a page in a magazine, newspaper, or this book to experiment with. Make sure it is on a flat surface, not balanced upright in your hands.

The first method is *pen down* (the other is *pen across*). Take a closed-top pen, not a pencil, and place it vertically on top of and in the center of the paragraph you are going to read. Your eyes are a line or two under the pen tip. Push the pen down as you begin reading, stopping your eyes only two, maybe three, times on each line, seeing more at a glance. Remember to use key words, phrases, or key phrases to help you go even faster. As you get accustomed to the method, try moving the pen a little faster.

In the pen across method, you place the pen in a horizontal position above the line you are going to start reading. Cover the words you already read and leave open where you are going. This is similar to the white card method.

Gauge Your Attitude

Let's take an attitude check. Write down or mentally fill in the blank of the following statement:

I am a(n) _____ reader.

Is your reading attitude changing?

 Pit Stop: Tip of the Day

Leaf through a magazine looking for advertisements. Choose one and create a mental dialogue with the advertiser. What is he trying to tell or sell you? How does he do it? What do you think his hidden strategy is for getting you to buy? The more you practice this healthy skepticism, the better you will become at asking thought-provoking questions in other reading contexts. Your answers will help you become a more informed, critical thinker.

Day 7 will continue to give you tips and strategies on how to take a large pile of reading material and select and make decisions based on its value, your time, and interest. You will also learn how to control the incoming flow of your reading material so it becomes more quality, not quantity.

Reducing the Pileup

Pileups are possible during any car race. This may happen because several cars are trying to maneuver out of the way of a slower car, the conditions on the track make for slippery driving, or there are just too many cars grouped together. These reasons are similar to why you might have a reading pileup: You may be reading too slowly, not reading on the best track, or feeling daunted by the amount in your reading pile.

You may be in a reading pileup situation right now. And you would probably like to know how to get out of it and how to avoid getting into it again. But before we get into the solutions to this problem, it's good to know why a reading pileup occurs.

Personal Contributors to the Reading Pile

Over the years, I have uncovered several popularly held attitudes and misconceptions that ultimately contribute to the increasing height of a reading pile. They are:

- I'll get to it later.

- If I am reading, then I am not working.
- I need to read everything I receive.
- I need to remember everything I read.
- I need this for my professional or personal development.

Let's look at each of these attitudes and misconceptions a little more carefully.

- **I'll get to it later.** When you receive reading material, usually you don't have time at the moment to stop what you are doing to read it. So you may put it on a pile called "later." You say, "Oh, I'll get to it later." But "later" rarely comes and the pile only gets bigger.

- **If I am reading, then I am not working.** After working with business professionals for several years, it became clear to me that many of them feel as if reading isn't part of their job during work hours. It's something they still need to do but they are not comfortable reading at work. They believe that reading at work looks like they are goofing off. Though in all likelihood no one's boss ever said that reading wasn't allowed at work, many employees believe that the boss would prefer them to read outside work hours. Where better, though, to get great business ideas and ways to stay current or surpass the competition than through relevant reading?

- **I need to read everything I receive.** People believe they need to read everything that comes in the mail or enters their in basket or e-mail box. If you act accordingly and really read it all, you will not have much time for the rest of your life! Reality dictates that you do not need to nor should you read it all.

- **I need to remember everything I read.** This comes directly from school experience. After all, you were tested on everything you read, right? In the real world, however, you are not officially tested on everything you read unless you are a student. You are sometimes responsible for sharing what you read with others but mostly what you comprehend from reading is for your own personal or professional benefit.

Many untrained readers continue to approach their reading just like they did when they were in school: They try to memorize everything before they even know what the reading is about. The process of memorizing in and of itself is a mechanical process of trying to imprint information on the brain for short-term recall. Whatever information studied is only available to you for a few days, at most. After several days, the details are almost all forgotten. It makes for an unnecessarily slow, tedious, and unrewarding experience for most reading requirements you have.

The absolute best way to remember what you read is to create an excellent retrieval system either electronically or on paper. This takes the pressure off feeling like you have to remember everything. Most times, you don't know which information is needed or when it will be used. It is unrealistic to believe you can recall in detail a piece of material you read a few months ago or last year. For the material I read that I suspect I will need in the future, I pre-view it, then read only those sections that interest me. I then effectively highlight it, identifying only key words, and/or write notes in the margin. Finally, I file it away in a labeled folder. I am thrilled when I go back to the folder, magazine, or book at a later time, and though I may not remember reading it, I see my highlights and margin notes. I have saved myself time and energy by having this memory system.

- **I need this for my professional or personal development.** If you want to continually improve yourself you should use reading as a means for learning. However, you don't need to gather and read everything ever written on a topic. When I became pregnant with my first child, I began searching for related magazines and books on parenting. Trust me when I say there is a massive amount of information out there. To narrow it down, I spoke to friends and experienced parents and found out what they had read. I went to the library and to the bookstore. I pre-viewed books on the shelf to find those that spoke to me, then I read just the parts that interested me. I became more confident about parenting just from what I chose to read; I certainly didn't need to read everything written on the topic to feel this confidence.

  As a sole proprietor of a business, I not only have to be an excellent speaker and trainer, but I also need to know how to use and maintain a computer, keep track of my income and expenses, organize my office, manage accounts receivable and payable, market and sell my services, and so on. I attribute most of my business success to what I have learned from reading selectively. You, too, can learn more in less time by reading.

 ## Fast Tracks:
Triage Your Reading Pile

Your reading pile can benefit from what emergency room physicians do every day—triage incoming patients. This means they sort people into groups based on their need for immediate treatment. You, too, can prioritize and select your reading material from highest to lowest priority using various methods.

To start, do you know what's actually in your pile? Where does it all come from? You need to know what you have before you know what you can get rid of. Review the six strategies below and see which ones you think you can use right away.

1. **Unsubscribe and get off distribution lists.** If you receive unsolicited e-mail newsletters, follow the simple directions at the end of the communication to get off the mailing list. If you are on a distribution list, either electronically or on paper, find out how to get off. The more you unsubscribe, the less unwanted or unnecessary reading material you receive.

2. **Pre-view everything!** Remember that pre-viewing (Day 5) is a great weeding tool. Using this technique, it takes only a short time to decide whether a piece of reading material is worth your time and what to focus your attention on.

3. **Photocopy or cut out articles.** When reading material such as magazines or professional journals arrives, quickly pre-view the table of contents to locate just the articles you want to read. If time does not permit you to read them at that moment, cut or tear the article out or photocopy it and discard the magazine. A small pile of handpicked articles is much more appealing to tackle than a huge stack of magazines or newspapers.

4. **Use self-adhesive notes.** Instead of earmarking pages, bending the corner of the page down, which then gets unbent most of the time, place a self-adhesive note so it sticks out of the top or side of the pages you want to

return to. You can write the topic or a few key words on the note for easy referencing.

5. **Keep a table of contents notebook.** If you receive a professional journal or even something like a food magazine that you like to keep for referencing, then photocopy the table of contents. Place it in a notebook according to the date. If you have more than one journal or publication, place a divider in the notebook separating the contents. When it comes time to look for a specific topic or piece of information, you save time by flipping through the notebook instead of each individual journal or magazine.

6. **Throw away junk mail.** When your mail arrives, stand over the trash can. Look at the return address and postage. Immediately throw away any solicitations you know you don't want. If the stamp or postage is less than twenty-one cents, then it was mailed bulk rate and is probably something you didn't ask for and don't want.

Try writing to this address to remove your name from unsolicited mailing lists. Include your name, home address, your polite request, and your signature.

Mail Preference Service
The Direct Marketing Association
P.O. Box 9008
Farmingdale, NY 11735-9008

In about three months, you should see a reduction in the unsolicited mail you receive at home. For more information, contact the Mail Preference Service at the address above for their consumer tip sheet. You can also check out www.privatecitizen.com for more options to reduce junk mail, or register with Junkbusters at http://www.junkbusters.com.

To get your name removed from all the current lists sold by the big three credit-gathering organizations (Equifax, Trans Union, and Experian—formerly TRW), call a program called OptOut at their automated toll-free number: 1-888-567-8688. You will probably still get some junk mail, however, as companies and organizations who previously purchased your name from these and other lists will not necessarily be notified.

Finding Time Nuggets

Making time to read is a great way to decrease the size of your reading pile. But there are only 24 hours in a day and you may believe that each hour is accounted for with sleep, work, school, errands, and so on. You may want to take a closer look. Some people think it's impossible to make more time in a day. Not true. What it really takes is accurate tracking of how you spend your time and reflection about how you want to make the most of your time.

I always devote one segment of my workshop to time management. During the discussion, I suggest to my participants that they complete a Daily Time Log for one week. You can create a Daily Time Log by taking a piece of paper and writing down one side of the paper fifteen-minute or thirty-minute intervals, from the time you wake up in the morning until you go to bed at night. Of course, each day may be different. For example, let's say you get up at 6:00 and leave for work at 7:15. Your time log should indicate what you did during that hour and fifteen minutes, such as getting up, showering and dressing, preparing and eating breakfast, and five minutes of reading the newspaper. Throughout the day continue to write all your activities such as commuting time, meetings, appointments, time spent watching TV or talking on the phone, and so on.

Although you already feel the constraints on your time from career and personal obligations, it is well worth your time to perform this exercise for one week.

Once your week is completed, try to determine how much time you spent doing each activity. Some areas you may have to calculate include the number of hours you spent sleeping, preparing and eating meals, commuting, watching TV, surfing the Web, or doing housework. When you are done you will have a clearer picture of how your time is spent. If the total falls under twenty-four hours, try to figure out where the rest of the time went.

Now look at your log. Is your time being spent how you want it to? Or is there too much time spent doing activities of little interest to you? Ideally, when you look at your log, you should feel happy and satisfied that your time is being well spent.

To find more reading time, review your log and look for the following:

- **Unaccounted for time.** This is the most logical place to build in more reading time.

- **Time-robbing activities.** For example, watching TV, talking on the phone, or surfing the Net. You may want to spend less time doing these activities in order to create more time for reading.

- **Time when you can multitask.** For example, you can read while commuting or waiting for meetings to start or appointments to arrive. Remember to always carry reading materials with you, since you never know when you'll have a few free moments.

- **Time you may have set aside to read but that is not the time of day you feel most alert.** You can read more in less time just by planning to read at the times when your brain is most awake.

- **Time you think you can squeeze in a few minutes.** If you usually eat lunch in a cafeteria, which is often noisy, you may want to eat at your desk or find a quieter place so as to be able to include some reading.

Finding time to read does not mean you have to schedule it at the same time every day. It means reading whenever and as often as possible. My husband, who is a certified financial planner, receives a lot of newspapers and magazines on a regular basis. Keeping abreast in his field is important to him and his clients. What seems to work well for him is that about every two weeks (sometimes it ends up to be once a month) he gathers all his reading material together and spends a few hours going through whatever he hadn't had the chance to look over during the course of the two weeks. When he emerges from his reading session, I can see the satisfaction on his face as he carries his small handful of torn-out articles (his keepers) and puts the rest in the recycle bin.

 Time Trial No. 7

Once again, it's time to test your engine. It should take you five minutes or less. On the following practice reading, experiment with some of the information you have learned about. Try using key words, phrases, key phrases, or a pacer. Ensure an appropriate environment for uninterrupted successful reading.

1. **Pre-view the reading first.** Time yourself for a maximum of only thirty seconds, allowing yourself to quickly look at the introduction, the first sentences of the paragraphs, and the questions you will be answering.

2. **Time yourself.** Now see how long it takes you to read the passage "The Ties That Bind" below. Write your total time in minutes and seconds in the space provided at the end of the reading.

The Ties That Bind

By John D. Whitman

"Nice work on this," Gilchrist said. He leaned back against the round table with the ease of a man who owned not only the furniture, but the building that housed it.

"Thanks, Mr. Gilchrist."

"You know, I gotta tell you, when you first came on board, I had my concerns. I knew you had the wife, two kids."

The wife. The two kids. At the office, Max's thoughts were only of business, and the unexpected mention of his home life jarred him.

"I mean, you've gotta have those commitments, they're the most important thing," Gilchrist admitted. "But you're the only family man on the fast track here, and I was afraid your focus . . ."

"I'm lucky enough to have a family who supports me," Max interjected.

"Good, because I'm looking around for a number two, Max, and it might be you."

Max floated back to his office, riding those words like winged sandals. He picked up his phone and pressed 1 on his speed dial.

"Twentieth Century Fox. Joan Kelly's office."

"Is the twenty-first-century fox in?" he asked.

The voice on the other end smiled. "Hey, Mr. Kelly. One minute, please."

Max heard a click that indicated he was being forwarded. Joan picked up and said "Hi" from her car phone. "How'd the meeting go?"

"Supercalifragilistic," he said. "The old man is dropping hints."

"You're a star," Joan said.

"But it means follow-up. I think I'm going to be late."

Pause. The sound of the world rushing by, another world somewhere at the other end of the digital connection, a world with other problems, other deadlines, their enormity communicated only by the length of the pause and then two words. "The kids."

"I know," he said. "But I don't think I can make it if I'm gonna get this report done. Can you go?"

Another pause. At the other end of the line, Joan Kelly was hurtling through the Cahuenga Pass, leaving Burbank, heading to a lunch meeting at Citrus. In the gaps between the billboards and apartment buildings, she caught glimpses of sun-baked grass on the hillsides. The trees looked archaic, like something out of her elementary school history class. She'd studied California history when she was a kid. She drove past the American Legion Hall with its cannon in the front, and recalled that Cahuenga Pass in 1845 had been the site of Los Angeles' only battle.

She sighed, surrendering. "I'll try."

Mark your reading time here: _____ (minutes) _____ (seconds).

3. **Respond to statements.** Immediately answer the following statements to the best of your ability WITHOUT looking back at the reading. Estimate the number of answers you believe are correct and put the number in the blank provided.

Comprehension Statements

Without looking back at the reading passage, respond to the following statements by indicating whether the statement is True (T), False (F), or Not Discussed (N).

_____ 1. Max's boss does not have a family.

_____ 2. Max's boss is concerned that Max's fast track career might be derailed by his family.

_____ 3. Max has a wife and three kids.

_____ 4. Max's last name is Gilchrist.

_____ 5. Number 1 on Max's speed dial connects him to his wife's office.

_____ 6. Max's wife works as a secretary for Twentieth Century Fox.

_____ 7. It can be inferred that Max's wife has a busy career of her own.

_____ 8. Max's boss told him he couldn't attend his kids' after-school event.

_____ 9. Max's wife wishes she hadn't given the house-keeper the day off.

_____ 10. Max feels lucky to have a family that supports him.

Now, estimate how many of these answers you believe you have correct out of ten _____.

4. **Check your responses.** Turn to the Answer Key on page 201. If you have any incorrect, mark the correct response and return to the reading passage to try to understand where you had a problem.

5. **Figure your comprehension percentage.** Add the total number of correct responses you have and multiply by

10. Write your comprehension percentage in your Personal Progress chart on page 205.

6. **Figure your Words per Minute.** Look at your reading time and round off the seconds to the nearest 10-second mark. Turn to the Words per Minute chart on page 207 and find your Words per Minute next to your reading time. Write your Words per Minute in your Personal Progress chart.

7. **Track your Time Trial scores.** Go to your Personal Progress chart and make sure you've recorded your Words per Minute, comprehension percentage, and the date you did the exercise. It's also helpful to document other details such as time of day, any preoccupations, strategies used, and so on.

Tips on Finding Time Nuggets While Waiting

How many times do you find yourself waiting in line at the grocery store or sitting in a doctor's office? These are two great examples of time pockets to make more reading time. For example, here are some pointers to help you speed-read a magazine during a time pocket.

- Choose your magazine based on either the title or the cover articles.

- Of course, choose the one that holds the most interest for you.

- Quickly review the table of contents looking for the cover articles that interest you. Also, look for other articles you may want to look at if time allows.

• Turn to the first article that interests you. Then pre-
  view it. Read the first paragraph or two, then read the
  first sentences of paragraphs. Look at illustrations,
  captions, and other features such as sidebars or boxes
  that stand out. Depending on your wait time, decide
  whether to read the article in more detail or move on to
  the next article.

• If you run out of time, buy the magazine and bring it
  home! Or ask the receptionist at the doctor's office to
  photocopy the article or whether you might be allowed
  to take the magazine home. I get the magazines for my
  training programs from my generous dentist, chiro-
  practor, and hairdresser. They usually go through and
  get rid of their stacks every few months because they,
  too, are overloaded.

 ## Turbo Comprehension: How to Read Your Newspaper Before You Reach Your Destination

Wouldn't it be great to actually finish your morning newspaper before arriving at work? If you commute by train, bus, or
carpool, it's possible. Obviously the longer the commute
time, the better your chances. However, even on short com-
mutes, you can still get a lot of information in a little amount
of time.

Your mind-set when reading a newspaper can greatly affect
how quickly and effectively you read. Try approaching your
newspaper reading with the same kind of time pressure you
have when reading a report that will be discussed at a meeting
in two hours. A self-imposed time limit for your newspaper
reading helps ensure completion of the task.

Many of the techniques already discussed in this book can be applied to reading a newspaper quickly:

- Purpose and responsibility.
- Pre-view.
- Skim and scan.
- Key words, phrases, and pacers.

- **Define your purpose and responsibility.** For example, your purpose may be to stay current on local and world events, or on topics relevant to your field of expertise, learning new information on topics such as business, real estate, the arts, and so on.

- **Pre-view!** This is best accomplished by looking at one section of the paper at a time, instead of the entire paper—particularly the Sunday edition if you plan to catch up on it on your way to work Monday morning. Put aside the advertising circulars so you have the meat of the paper in your hands.

    To pre-view a newspaper section, quickly thumb through it, reading the date, section title, index, headlines, and captions under photos. Mentally make a note of which articles are relevant to your purpose. Also mark articles that pique your interest and relate to your purpose by either putting a dot next to the headline with a marker, or writing a key word or phrase in the margin next to the article.

- **Skim and scan.** Once you pre-view a section, systematically work through the paper, skimming and scanning your chosen articles looking for information relevant to your purpose.

- **Key words, phrases, and pacers.** Remember to use key words, phrases, and pacers to optimize your reading.

Use the Commuter Fold

Reading a newspaper in the confined spaces of your commuter seat is a challenging maneuver. The commuter fold helps you fold, hold, and turn the pages of your paper to reduce your required reading space. Take a newspaper and follow the steps below.

- Unfold the paper so the front page is in front of you.

- Fold the paper in half length-wise so the back page halves touch one another. Read what you want from the left side of page 1, then flip the paper over to read the right side of page 1.

- Take hold of the bottom right corner of page 1 in your left hand and fold it back. The right side of page 1 will be touching the left side of page 1. You will be viewing the left side of page 2. If you turn your whole paper over, you will be looking at the right side of page 3.

- To view the right side of page 2, take hold of the fold of page 2 and fold it back so that the left of page 2 meets the right of page 3.

Keep in mind that a newspaper has nearly as many words as a novel, so remember you can't, nor should you, read it all, but you can choose your material wisely.

How to Speed-Read Written Business Communications

Written business communications come in many different lengths and formats. Some examples include memos, letters, reports, policies, FYI's (for your information), and so on. Remember, speed reading is not one fast speed, but rather degrees of slow and fast. You consciously decide which speed you will use, depending on:

- The subject of the communication.
- Its relevance to your current tasks.
- Who sent it.
- Your time frame.
- Your knowledge level of the topic.
- The author's writing style.
- Whether a response is needed.

No matter the type of written communication, be sure to pre-view it for general content, use key words, phrases, or key phrases while reading, and a pacer (hand or card method).

Special Tips for Speed-Reading E-Mail

Nowadays, e-mail is de rigueur in the business world and is used ubiquitously to correspond with employees, clients, customers, and so on. Here are four tips to help you manage your e-mail in box.

- **Look at who it is sent to as well as who sent it.** Are you one of many who received this e-mail or was it only sent to your attention? If it was a group e-mail, then chances are greater it is more an FYI than a crucial business communication. If your e-mail program allows, set up a preference that puts e-mails from certain senders in a specific folder. For example, all e-mails from your boss will automatically go into your "Boss" folder. So each day when you check your in box, immediately go to that folder first.

- **Look at the subject line.** Ideally, the subject line of an e-mail should give you an indication of the topic of the message. Encourage senders to be specific as to what they want you to know before opening the mail. Some examples are:

  RE: Your input on meeting agenda needed on 11th for 12th.

  RE: How is the budget proposal coming?

  RE: Thanks for your quick response on the sales meeting.

  By reading the e-mail's subject line, you'll be able to determine whether you can read the e-mail later, just skim it, or delete it without reading it all.

- **Pre-view.** Some e-mail programs let you pre-view the communication, which allows you a quick peek at the content to decide whether or not you want to spend your time on it now, later, or never.

- **Use speed techniques.** You can use the key word, phrase, or key phrase technique on screen. Pacers, however, are more challenging. Instead of using your arrow key to read line by line, try using the mouse to scroll to the section of text you want to read, read the entire section, then scroll to the next section of text you want to read, scrolling right past sections you want to skip.

 **Start Your Engines:
The Open Hand Wiggle**

Here's another pacer to try. The Open Hand Wiggle is a comfortable movement for the hand. Choose a page in a magazine, newspaper, or this book. Make sure the reading material is placed firmly on a reading surface, not held up in your hands.

Open either hand with your fingers extended outward and your palm facing the page. Place your hand over the text with the middle finger centered in the middle of the column. Slowly slither your hand in an S shape down the column, moving down and across a few lines at a time. Your hand should lightly touch the page as it moves. Your eyes move from left to right. You can use key words, phrases, or key phrases to help you go even faster. You are to follow your middle finger down the page. As you become more accustomed to this method, try moving your hand a little faster.

How to Speed-Read a Web Site

Whether you are a student doing research, a professional researching a new project or your competitors, or an avid home surfer working on your next vacation or home improvement project, you know you can find helpful and valuable information on the Web. However, you also know that sometimes you spend more time than you need finding what you want.

Jakob Nielsen of the Nielsen Norman Group, noted researcher about the Web, has put appropriate names to what Web users do: forage and consume. Web foragers are information searchers who ruthlessly seek out what they're looking for. They are focused and hungry for information and don't want to spend any more time than necessary locating it. They do not read anything in its entirety at first. Instead, they skim, looking for generally what is there and then scan, looking for specific information. Once they have found it, then they consume the information, or skim for more detail. This behavior pattern shows Web users naturally perform useful speed reading techniques.

Here are some tips to help you limit the number of Web

sites you have to forage through to gain key information
without going cross-eyed:

- **Start your search with Google or Yahoo.** By these well-
  known, commercially-backed search engines generally
  means you will get more dependable results. They are
  more likely to be well-maintained and upgraded when
  necessary to keep pace with the growing web.

- **Know the difference between a search engine and a
  directory.** A search engine is a computer program that
  recognizes the entered keywords to locate specific web
  pages. It checks the complete text of web pages for the
  keyword or words. Search engines don't search the
  entire Internet, rather they search the pages in their
  database. There are thousands of search engines. Some
  popular ones include:

  - Altavista.com
  - Google.com
  - MSN.com
  - Yahoo.com
  - Ask.com
  - AOL.com

  A directory is a subject guide developed by people
  rather than automated software and usually organized
  by major topics and subtopics. Directory-based sites
  tend to give fewer results but typically more useful ones.

  - Yahoo.com
  - Google.com
  - Infomine.com
  - AlltheWeb.com
  - Lycos.com
  - About.com

- **Learn how to perform effective Boolean searches.**
Though search engines may find what you need on
your first inquiry, it is still helpful to know how to
narrow down your search results. Boolean searches refer
to using the most efficient search terms that you can to
locate what you are searching for, usually by employing
words such as "and" or "+". Search engines will then
locate sites that include the words or terms you've
coupled together. For example, when you enter
"Shakespeare" as your search term, more than 48
million sites will come up! Use a Boolean search in
quotes to narrow your choices to something like
"Shakespeare + regional festivals."

- **View only the top 10 percent (or less) of your search
results.** Many search engines prioritize the sites they
find for you—those that most closely match your search
criteria appear first. You may choose to view only these
sites, then move on to another search engine or restate
your search criteria with a different Boolean search.

- **Consider clicking the ads next to your search engine
results.** Many serious product and service providers pay
to have their company listed on the same page your
search results are listed. Patronize those that seem most
appropriate to your needs.

- **Use a home page like a table of contents.** Most Web
sites have a home page with links to various topics on
other pages of the site. Use only those you need.

- **Bookmark your favorite sites.** This will save you time
when you want to go back and look for information.
TIP: When you save your favorites, consider writing
your password next to the saved name of the site so you
don't lose it!

- **Use speed reading techniques.** You can use the key word, phrase, or key phrase technique on screen. Get proficient at skimming and scanning.

- **Set a time frame.** Seasoned users know that spending time on the Web can easily take up valuable time. If you set a specific time frame for Web searching, you will be more inclined to work more efficiently and not get side-tracked.

- **Resist printing—read more on screen.** You will save valuable time by reading the text on screen rather than taking the time to print a document. Also, it will cut down on your reading pileup.

Making More Time: How to Manage Monthly or Weekly Tasks

Let's face it, there are not enough hours in a day to accomplish those time-consuming tasks such as preparing a weekly dinner menu or grocery shopping and still have time to read. However, if you devise a system and stick with it, not only will those tasks be less time consuming, but you will have more reading time. For example, here is a system for managing your bills to make more time for reading.

For most people paying bills is a boring and time-consuming activity. But it can become less painful if you become aware of your bill-paying pattern and look for better, faster, more efficient ways of doing it.

Many people find that using their computer to pay bills saves a great deal of time. You can easily track your accounts and print your checks on the computer, saving a lot of time writing and calculating. Once you print out the checks, all you have left to do is sign them, put the checks and bills into envelopes, put on stamps, and address the envelopes. Some people take it a step further and never handle a check; your bank wires the money for your bills with the click of a mouse. No signature, stamps, or checks.

Depending on how you choose to pay your bills, you may find a good idea in the following suggestions that will save you time:

- **Prepare the bills as soon as you open them.** Open the bill, quickly review and discard the excess pages, then paper-clip the bill and the return payment envelope together. Put the bills in a large manila envelope or folder titled "Bills Payable" and keep it in a place that will be a constant reminder for you.

- **Mark the envelope with the due date.** With every bill you write "date to pay" on a sticky note on the return envelope. Make sure to keep the bills in the order of their due dates to make it easier when it comes time to pay them.

- **Create a list of your monthly bills.** Make twelve copies, one for each month. Include the name of the company and in the space next to it write the amount payable and due date. When you sit down to pay your bills, either by computer or hand, you know exactly how much you owe and you can expedite the check-writing process.

I cut off two hours of bill-paying time by using the above ideas. Now wouldn't you like that nice time nugget for reading? Try devising your own time management system for daily, weekly, or monthly tasks that you think are eating up too much time.

Gauge Your Attitude

Let's take an attitude check. Write down or mentally fill in the blank of the following statement:

I am a(n) _____ reader.

Is your reading attitude changing?

 ## Pit Stop: Tip of the Day

If you want to really push yourself with these faster reading strategies, try using a metronome. A metronome is a time-keeping device used by musicians. It can be set at different speeds and makes a tick sound each time the ticker goes back and forth. I suggest using reading material with narrow columns such as a newspaper or magazine for this exercise. Begin by setting the metronome at a slow rate to gauge your ability to read it. Your objective is to start at the beginning of the first line on the first tick and then reach the end of the line at the second tick, go to the beginning of the next line on the third tick, and so on. It is challenging to get into a strict reading rhythm but it is a great exercise for helping you develop speed. As you become more comfortable and find you are reading faster than the ticks, increase speed on the metronome.

In Day 8, you will learn about your hypothetical gear shift, which includes the overdrive features skimming, scanning, and skipping. You will also look at the issues related to reading on a computer screen.

Fine-Tuning Your Reading Speed

When you are on the highway, you can drive fifty-five miles per hour or in some places sixty-five or more. But during rush hour, you probably can't. And driving down Main Street in your town might be faster at midnight than midday. There are many factors that determine the speed of your vehicle, such as time of day, traffic, weather conditions, construction zones, and so on. Race car drivers adjust their speed, too, depending on track conditions. Being aware of these conditions and adjusting your driving speed accordingly, you ensure a safe and efficient journey.

Today you will look at your hypothetical gear shift and the speed control you have with your reading. Knowing your purpose (Day 3) and applying pre-viewing (Day 5) are the key factors for determining your overdrive speeds: skimming, scanning, or skipping. You'll look at the differences between reading on paper and the computer. Also you'll get another opportunity to gauge your reading attitude and take a Time Trial for tracking your progress.

Your Control Box: The Gear Shift

Race cars have a gear shift. That's because adjusting your speed is much more efficient with a standard gear shift than with an automatic. You have greater control over the vehicle and more power to get where you want to go at the speed you want to get there. Efficient readers have a gear shift that allows them flexibility to change gears depending upon the conditions of the road or driver.

In car racing, there is a flag waver who informs the driver when to speed up and slow down. If it's okay for the driver to speed up, a green flag is waved. If the driver needs to slow down, a yellow flag is waved.

You have your own reading flags that help you know when it's safe to speed up or slow down. Many of these signals will be familiar to you from previous chapters—learn to pay attention to how each affects your speed.

- **Purpose and responsibility.** If your purpose is to get the gist of your material, then you can speed up; if your purpose is to study or memorize, then you need to slow down.

- **Pre-viewing.** Pre-viewing provides you with background knowledge. This familiarity helps speed up your reading. Without it you spend more time trying to figure out the reading's meaning and the result is that you read more slowly or read material you don't need to read.

- **Background knowledge.** Any reading content that is familiar or has easy vocabulary speeds you up. Any content that is unfamiliar or difficult vocabulary slows you down.

- **Noise level.** You read faster and more efficiently in a place that has a noise level you are comfortable with. Most adults prefer a quiet location; so a noisy location may slow you down.

- **Distractions and interruptions.** Taking control over your distractions and interruptions while reading will help you read faster and usually with better focus and comprehension. If you allow your kids, other people, the telephone, e-mail, or other distractions to interrupt you, your reading naturally slows down and results in reduced focus and comprehension.

- **Time factor.** If you are reading to meet a deadline, you have great reason to speed up. If you have all the time in the world, then you have the option of reading quickly or slowly.

- **Time of day.** Knowing your peak, or awake, times of day, and reading at those times, helps you speed up your reading. Trying to read at your nonpeak, or sleepier, times of day slows you down.

- **Physical condition.** If you are well rested, not hungry, in comfortable clothes, feeling well, and so on, then you are able to read faster than if you are exhausted, starving, wearing constricting clothes, or ill. I poll my classes and ask how many feel well rested most of the time. Not many raise their hands. If you feel tired most of the time, I do not want you to think you are condemned to reading slowly your whole life. This would be a good time to use some of the speed-up strategies to help you get through the material quickly. And if you read faster, you'll have more time for sleep.

- **Using a speed technique.** If you use an active reading strategy such as key words, phrases, key phrases, or a pacer, you read faster. If you don't, you won't.

- **Location.** If you are reading for school or for work, then being in a place the brain is used to working, such as a desk or table, helps you read with more speed.

- **Temperature and lighting.** A room where the lighting is adequate for you and it's neither too hot nor too cold is more conducive to faster reading than one with inadequate lighting or an uncomfortable temperature.

- **Interest.** People differ about how quickly they read when they are interested in the material. What do you do? Do you speed up or slow down? Some readers prefer to get to the meat, the main gist of the reading, while others like to chew everything slowly and read a piece of material from start to finish.

- **Column width and print size.** Do you know if you prefer narrow or wide columns? Which font size do your eyes prefer? Generally speaking, wider columns are more challenging to read than narrow columns. However, pacers can help with any column width. Reading material that is agreeable to your eye speeds you up. If not, you tend to slow down.

- **Author's style.** If the author's style engages you, then chances are you will enjoy what you are reading and read it faster. If you dislike the author's style, then you will think about how much you don't like what you are reading and slow down.

You might be thinking, "It would be great to read with all of these green flags up at the same time. How can I do it?" Yes, it would be great but it would also be unusual and unrealistic. The idea is not to strive for perfection here, but rather to take as much control over your reading material, reading time, and physical environment as possible to make your reading experience as efficient and as effective as possible.

Through trial and error, you will figure out which conditions matter and which don't. You will become a pro at getting the most out of the material you read in the least amount of time. Be aware though that even a pro has a bad day but it doesn't mean he can't race. It just means he has to take better control of his gear shift depending upon the current track conditions. Let's say you have to read a proposal for your business meeting the following day. No problem. Except you are really tired. What do you do? Either you can take a short nap or get up early the next morning to read the report. I always suggest reading at a table or desk with good lighting but never read anything extremely important when you are very tired. You will daydream a lot, have a hard time following the author's train of thought, and you won't retain what you read.

Skim, Scan, or Skip

Skimming, scanning, and skipping function like the overdrive on your gear shift. They are the three most used reading techniques. They might best be described as techniques for *not* reading. The fundamental skill in each lies in knowing when and how to do it without missing what you need to comprehend from the reading. As with so many reading skills, the selectivity is found in your reading purpose and responsibility (Day 3).

Skimming

Use skimming when you are looking for the general or main ideas of a reading. Skimming is a deliberate method of reading that results in a solid overview with selected details. You skim when your purpose is:

- To pull out the main ideas from a large amount of material.

- To test whether a passage can be safely skipped.

- To locate material that needs to be read thoroughly.

- To obtain a general, bird's-eye view without the mastery of detail that thorough reading provides.

Appropriate material for skimming includes, but is not limited to, Web sites, e-zines, magazines, newspapers, nonfiction books, and manuals.

Skimming is similar to pre-viewing with one difference. You now add more to the process than just reading the first sentence of a paragraph. Though the first sentence usually gives you the main idea of a paragraph, many times you get important details in other parts of the paragraph *without reading it all.* If you feel the first sentence is not helpful, add a phrase or two from the second sentence. Then let your eyes *quickly* swing down the rest of that paragraph looking for names, dates, numbers, and any other details that relate to your reading purpose. Occasionally, if the first sentence plus these details do not give you enough about what the paragraph contains, then, and only then, should you read the last sentence of the paragraph. Continue doing the same for the next paragraph and so on. To make this process work and to avoid reading it all, you must proceed with a very clear idea of what you are looking for.

This technique takes more time to describe than do. You

HOW TO SKIM

Usually the first paragraph will be read at average speed all the way through. It often contains an introduction or overview of what will be talked about.

Sometimes, however, the second paragraph contains the introduction or overview. In the first paragraph the author might just be "warming up" or saying something clever to attract attention.

Reading a third paragraph completely might be unnecessary but ... ... the main idea is usually contained in the opening sentence ... ... topic sentence ... ...

Besides the first sentence the reader should get some but not all the detail from the rest of the paragraph ... ... names ... ... dates ... ...

This tells you nothing ... ...

... ... hence sometimes the main idea is in the middle or at the end of the paragraph.

Some paragraphs merely repeat ideas ... ...

Occasionally the main idea can't be found in the opening sentence. The whole paragraph must then be read.

Then leave out a lot of the next paragraph ... ... to make up time ... ...

Remember to keep up a very fast rate ... ... 800 wpm ... ...

Don't be afraid to leave out half or more of each paragraph ... ...

Don't get interested and start to read everything ... ... skimming is work ... ...

... ...

Lowered comprehension is expected ... ... 50% ... ... not too low

Skimming practice makes it easier ... ... gain confidence ... ...

Perhaps you won't get anything at all from a few paragraphs ... ... don't worry ... ...

Skimming has many uses ... ... reports ... ... newspapers ... ... supplementary ... ... text ... ...

The ending paragraphs might be read more fully as often they contain a summary.

Remember that the importance of skimming is to get only the author's main ideas at a very fast speed.

(Edward Fry, "How to Skim," from *Teaching Faster Reading: A Manual,* 1963, reprinted with the permission of Cambridge University Press, New York.)

must keep your skimming fast and flexible so it feels like you are sprinting on tiptoe down an obstacle course. On page 152 is an example of the eye movements involved in skimming. Move your eyes as quickly as possible to the words.

Fast Tracks: Skimming a Passage

Locate an article from a magazine or a chapter from a nonfiction book that you want to read. Decide on your purpose and responsibility. Your purpose could be as simple as wanting to try skimming and your responsibility is to find as much detail as possible, for your interest level, without reading it all. Follow the skimming passage presented on page 151 and in "How to Skim" above. Give yourself about fifteen to thirty seconds per page, even less if you are willing to get the most information in the least amount of time without reading it all. When you are done, evaluate your experience. Did you get the gist? Were you able to go fast enough? What would you do differently next time you skim? Remember, you will become skilled through trial and error.

Scanning

The opposite of skimming, scanning is used when you are looking for something specific, a particular piece of information. You probably scan all the time but may not realize that is what you are doing. Some examples of scanning are when you:

- Do research on the Internet.
- Look at the TV listings to see what time your favorite show is on.

- Look for a specific topic in an index or table of contents.
- Look for the baseball scores in a daily paper.
- Look up a phone number in a telephone book.

Frequently, readers skim *and* scan the same piece of material. In a newspaper, you might skim the headlines looking for a story that is of interest to you, then you may scan it looking for specific details such as who it concerns, when did it happen, or how much did it cost. On a retail Web site, you might skim the home page and links, getting the gist of what is offered and how the site is set up. You then go to a linked page scanning for a specific detail such as description of an item, cost, or availability.

The easiest way to become efficient at scanning is to place a pen or pencil vertically, from top to bottom, on the center of a column or page. Let your eyes make two stops per line of print, one to the left of the pen and one to the right. Narrower columns may permit one stop while wider columns may need three. Your scanning may be more accurate if you look at the white space between the lines rather than the lines themselves. Your attention is spread more evenly throughout your field of vision and not concentrated on single words.

Once you master scanning, you can stop putting the pen on the reading. The pen is meant to remind the untrained reader not to slip back into word-for-word reading.

Scanning can be done as quickly as 1,500 words per minute. This incredible speed is attributed to the fact you are looking for only one thing while not reading the rest.

Comprehension while scanning is either 100 percent or 0 percent. If you find what you are looking for and document it accurately, you get 100 percent. If you don't accurately find what you are looking for or don't document correctly, you get 0 percent.

Turbo Comprehension: Scanning

Here is a telephone list and a series of ten questions, or pieces of information, to look for from the listing. With the help of a pacer, your hand, or finger, pull your eyes down the page looking for the answer. Notice how your eyes distinguish information only when you stop them. Try using your peripheral vision to see above and below your stopping point. When you find the answer to a question, quickly and accurately document the answer, including first names and middle initials as shown. Since all have the same last name, save yourself time by not writing it down.

To really make it a challenge, time yourself. Read the questions carefully.

1. Whose phone number is 531-7379? _____

2. Who lives at 2 Grigg?_____

3. How many listings does 296 Palmer Hill Rd have? _____

4. What is the business phone of Joseph L. Hayes Jr? _____

5. Whose phone number is 661-3383?_____

6. Who lives at 182 Taconic Rd? _____

7. What is the phone number of 205 S Water? _____

8. What is the address of Richard A. Hayes? _____

9. Whose phone number is 868-1391? _____

10. Who lives at 795 Lake Ave? _____

868-5178 **Hayes A M** 56 Oak Ridge
532-7968 **Hayes Anne M Mrs** 80 Henry
632-1023 **Hayes Antique Shop** 179 Shore Rd
868-2933 **Hayes B E** 7 Gaston Farm Rd
629-9016 **Hayes Barbara S**

637-4810 **Hayes Basil & Christine** 10 Owenoke Way
637-8993 **Hayes Beryl** 296 Palmer Hill Rd
661-1248 **Hayes C** 790 Lake Av
637-4208 **Hayes C** Webb Colonial La
531-9084 **Hayes Christopher B** 4 Hawthorne
531-7379 **Hayes Claude H** 92 Bowman Dr
629-4785 **Hayes Clem** 83 Mason
531-0225 **Hayes & Co** 251 Mill
637-7561 **Hayes David** 5 Pilot Rock La
531-7321 **Hayes David J** 54 Mead Av
622-0279 **Hayes Davidson D** 58 Cliffdale Rd
868-1114 **Hayes Elizabeth C** North Maple
637-1286 **Hayes Francis S** 35 Marks Rd
868-6084 **Hayes Frank D** 14 Brookridge Dr
637-0635 **Hayes George & Kathi** 24 Lake Drive S
661-7175 **Hayes Geo R D** 133 Otter Rock Dr
531-4228 **Hayes Gwynne** 43 Deep Gorge Rd
637-8993 **Hayes Howard O Jr Dr** 296 Palmer Hill Rd
637-0848 **Hayes** - Children Phone 296 Palmer Hill Rd
629-2331 **Hayes J Bryan III** 10 Bolling Pl
637-1766 **Hayes J R** 34 Druid La
661-7187 **Hayes John F** Vinyrd La
868-1391 **Hayes John I** 91 Prospect
868-1995 **Hayes Joseph L III** 50 Bush Av
661-9283 **Hayes Jos L Jr** 141 Ovrik Dr
868-6800 **Hayes Joseph L Jr** rl est 32 Sherwood Pl
868-2892 **Hayes Joseph S** Tinker La
868-6800 **Hayes Josephine C** rl est 32 Sherwood Pl
531-5061 **Hayes K & R** 171 Henry
868-8376 **Hayes K R** 182 Taconic Rd
868-3800 **Hayes Karen L** atty 100 Fieldpoint Rd
531-1941 **Hayes Keith** 40 Nutmeg Dr
625-9443 **Hayes Ken** 16 Lexington Av
637-1687 **Hayes Lincoln A** 44 Laddins Rock Rd Old
698-0870 **Hayes Lou** 5 Ferris Dr

661-6856 **Hayes M V V** 6 Stanwich Rd
531-6025 **Hayes Marjorie** 1165 King
939-9307 **Hayes Martin** 11 Pearl Pt Chstr
629-2341 **Hayes Philip** 155 Field Pt Rd
625-0671 **Hayes Philip J** 2 Grigg
661-3383 **Hayes R E** 140 Field Point Rd
531-5061 **Hayes R & K** 171 Henry
531-8570 **Hayes Richard A** 6 Thistle La
531-7282 **Hayes Roger J** 15 Prospect St W
868-9198 **Hayes Staunton Jr** 184 Parsonage Rd
868-4826 **Hayes Sydney M** 795 Lake Av
531-6233 **Hayes Thos R** 205 S Water

Go to the Answer Key on page 201 and check your answers. If you took three minutes or less to do this exercise, then your scanning speed is quite good. If you had nine out of ten correct or a perfect score, then your accuracy is on target. If it took you more time or you got fewer correct, you need to pay attention to either your scanning speed or accuracy.

Skipping

Skipping means leaving something unread altogether. You skip when you realize at any point in your reading that the material is unnecessary, repetitive, or filler. A skilled reader accurately knows when it is safe and desirable to skip.

Skipping is a selective way to read. The key point when skipping is in what you *do* read, not what you leave out. You often are faced with numerous pieces of material that could be relevant to your purpose. If a portion of the material can be skipped how do you choose? You can skip reading altogether if:

- It contains nothing new.
- It covers nothing you need.
- It's too difficult.

If you read varied material on the same topic in newspapers, Web sites, and magazines you most likely are getting the same information presented in different ways. For example, just about every book and article on pregnancy discusses the importance of folic acid. If it's information you already know, you can skip it or read it again to reinforce what you already gained from the reading. Pre-viewing or skimming also helps you quickly identify areas you can safely skip.

To learn how to skim, scan, or skip effectively, you need to consider the following:

1. **Always identify your purpose for reading.** Remember that without knowing why you are on the road, you waste time, get lost, and become frustrated.

2. **Pre-view everything you read.** Pre-viewing gives you the background knowledge to decide whether the reading is worth your time and helps you refine your purpose.

3. **Overcome your fear of missing material.** There is more than enough reading material to last a lifetime and your job is to *q-u-i-c-k-l-y* find what is most valuable to you.

 ## Time Trial No. 8

Once again, it's time to test your engine. It should take you five minutes or less. Remember to add pre-viewing into the process.

On the following practice reading, experiment with some of the information you have learned about. Try using key words, phrases, key phrases, or a pacer. Ensure an appropriate environment for uninterrupted successful reading.

1. **Pre-view the reading first.** Time yourself for a maximum of only thirty seconds, allowing yourself to quickly look at the introduction, the first sentences of the paragraphs, and the questions you will be answering.

2. **Time yourself.** See how long it takes to read the passage "Books Join the Electronic Wave" below. Write your total time in minutes and seconds in the space provided at the end of the reading.

Books Join the Electronic Wave

By John D. Whitman

Today, I read a book that wasn't there.

Well, the text was there, but the book wasn't. You see, I have one of those electronic organizers called a personal digital assistant, or PDA. Not only does it keep track of my address book, it also provides a host of other functions. For example it has the ability to store books on its memory. And not just tiny books. This device, which fits into a shirt pocket, can hold the complete works of Shakespeare, novels by Charles Dickens, or the Bible. Now you can have *King Lear* in your carrying case, *Pickwick Papers* in your purse.

Now, I'm not a technology nerd. So my first reaction to learning about "e-books," as they're called, was "This is surely the end of civilization as we know it." So, just to be spiteful, I decided to try this e-book feature and downloaded F. Scott Fitzgerald's classic novel *The Great Gatsby*.

I quickly learned that my expectations were wrong: E-books are actually a wonderful tool for reading on the go. In fact, they remind me of a time when the words were more important than the printing. You see, what we call "writing" began as oral tradition, stories passed from generation to generation before the advent of written language. In Western culture, it wasn't until the Greeks borrowed writing from the Phoenicians that stories were set down on papyrus . . . er, paper. The works of Homer, in fact, marked the transition from oral to written culture, but those early "books" emphasized the words themselves rather than the written medium.

Before the invention of the printing press, handwritten books were so rare that they took on a value of their own. The monks who created many of these early works labored so carefully that we call their works "illuminated manuscripts" because of the glorious artwork inked onto every page. Even today, when books are printed quickly and inexpensively, they hold a place of reverence.

But, in truth, we revere the ideas and language, not the books themselves. Reading Fitzgerald's classic novel on a small, electronic screen, I was struck just as powerfully by his ideas and insights as I would have been if the words had been in ink. Just as Homer's *Odyssey* transcended the scrolls on which it was written, great writing rises above the electronic format. It doesn't matter whether the text is ink or ether; printed or digital: excellent writing makes for good reading.

Mark your reading time here: _____ (minutes) _____ (seconds).

3. **Respond to statements.** Immediately answer the following statements to the best of your ability WITHOUT looking back at the reading. Estimate the number of answers you believe are correct and put the number in the blank provided.

Comprehension Statements

Without looking back at the reading passage, respond to the following statements by indicating whether the statement is True (T), False (F), or Not Discussed (N).

_____ 1. A PDA is a professional digital assistant.

_____ 2. A PDA can store addresses.

_____ 3. Only technology nerds enjoy reading e-books.

_____ 4. An e-book screen is easier to read if the original text is taken from a hardcover book.

_____ 5. The author tried reading fiction on his small electronic screen.

_____ 6. When books are printed in electronic form, the language loses some of its power.

_____ 7. Before the printing press, monks hand wrote books called illuminated manuscripts.

_____ 8. E-books are less expensive than printed ones.

_____ 9. Only classical fiction is available on e-books.

_____ 10. It's not "books" we revere, rather the ideas and language.

Now, estimate how many of these answers you believe you have correct out of ten _____.

4. **Check your responses.** Turn to the Answer Key on page 202. If you have any incorrect, mark the correct response and return to the reading passage to try to understand where you had a problem.

5. **Figure your comprehension percentage.** Add the total number of correct responses you have and multiply by 10. Write your comprehension percentage in your Personal Progress chart on page 206.

6. **Figure your Words per Minute.** Look at your reading time and round off the seconds to the nearest 10-second mark. Turn to the Words per Minute chart on page 207 and find your Words per Minute next to your reading time. Write your Words per Minute in your Personal Progress chart.

7. **Track your Time Trial scores.** Go to your Personal Progress chart and make sure you've recorded your Words per Minute, comprehension percentage, and the date you did the exercise. It's also helpful to document

other details such as time of day, any preoccupations, strategies used, and so on.

Reading on a Computer Screen

Race car drivers, and all drivers in general, are likely to drive slower in unfamiliar territory, or terrain that is new to them. For readers, the same is true when navigating the unfamiliar or less-than-ideal terrain of reading from a computer screen. Anyone who has read on a computer screen intuitively knows it is not the same as reading on paper.

Research has shown that people experience a 30 percent reduction in speed when reading from a screen. So if your reading speed averages 250 words per minute on paper, your reading speed on a screen may go down to 175 words per minute. Also comprehension, concentration, and retention are reduced when reading from a computer screen. Extensive research by Paul Muter, from the psychology department at the University of Toronto, identified 24 reasons to partially explain why reading from a computer screen is not the same as on paper, some of which may be responsible for the decrease in speed, including:

- The distance between the reading material and the reader.
- Screen resolution.
- Characters per line.
- Left justification vs. full justification.
- Margin width.
- Posture of the reader.
- Familiarity with the medium.

- System response time.

These differences may also explain why people prefer to print longer documents from their screen to paper. Price Waterhouse Coopers, an accounting and business firm, recently conducted a study tracking the paper consumption in offices that began using e-mail and found a 40 percent increase in paper use. I partially attribute this increase to the reduction in reading speed and the overall comfort levels when reading from paper as opposed to reading from a computer screen.

You are going to have to get used to screen reading, however, because the technology is here to stay. According to researcher and on-screen speed reading specialist Pam Mullan, the best way to adapt to reading in the computer age is to rely less on printing done on paper, and practice reading from the screen.

To help people improve their on-screen reading comfort levels, Mullan suggests changing the font size and style for a positive impact on your screen-reading abilities. For readability, she suggests sans serif fonts such as Arial, Verdana, and Helvetica. Font size should not be smaller than twelve point, and not larger than eighteen point, but Mullan encourages individuals to try different styles and sizes to determine personal preferences.

Many of the skills already discussed for reading on paper can be applied to screen reading. Strategies such as reading key words, phrases, and key phrases help you increase your speed on screen. Purpose and responsibility apply to screen reading as much (if not more) as they do to paper reading. Pre-viewing is sometimes possible and skimming, scanning, and skipping are always an option.

One simple application for skipping involves managing your e-mail. For example, rather than opening e-mail that you know is junk mail from reading the subject line, immediately delete it, thus reducing unnecessary reading. Pacers, your hand, or a card, unfortunately are very awkward. See "Tip of the Day" below for an on-screen pacer suggestion. As more and more information becomes available electronically rather than on paper, you therefore need to apply as many tips and techniques as possible to improve your computer reading abilities.

If you didn't know already, READING ALL CAPITAL LETTERS IS VERY HARD ON THE EYES. SOME PEOPLE USE THEM WHEN THEY TYPE ON A SCREEN OR PAPER. IN THE COMPUTER TEXT WORLD, PEOPLE FEEL AS IF THEY ARE BEING SHOUTED AT WHEN SOMEONE WRITES IN ALL CAPITAL LETTERS. All capital letters also slows you down. So when you compose text on a computer, use standard upper- and lowercase letters for readability.

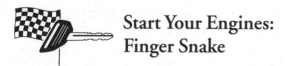 ## Start Your Engines: Finger Snake

The Finger Snake is similar to the Pull Down Center pacer introduced in Day 5. It works best on narrow-columned material. Choose a page in a magazine, newspaper, or this book to experiment with. Make sure to place it on a flat surface, not balanced upright in your hands. Pick the index finger of either hand. Place the finger in the center of the column under the first line of text. First understand the movement by pretending your finger is a snake and you are slithering it down the page. Your finger should move in a constant wide S pattern, starting on the right, then going toward the left and back to the right and so on. Do not zigzag your finger on every line, rather move your fingers a few lines down each time you move from one side to the other. Eventually you will be able to see and read more than one line at a time.

Once you understand the movement, add your eyes and brain to it. Have your finger go as slowly or as quickly as your eyes read each line from side to side. Try stopping your eyes only two or three times on each line, seeing more at a glance. Remember to use key words, phrases, or key phrases to help you go even faster. As you get more accustomed to the method, try moving your finger a little faster.

Gauge Your Attitude

Let's take an attitude check. Write down or mentally fill in the blank of the following statement:

I am a(n) _____ reader.

Is your reading attitude changing?

 ## Pit Stop: Tip of the Day

There are several computer programs available to help you learn how to develop your eye movements for faster reading on paper and on screen. I recommend AceReader. AceReader software is inexpensive and compatible for both PCs and Macs. After you load the software, you paste in your own text or use any of the two hundred preloaded reading drills and set the speed controls and word display to your choosing. You can download a thirty-day trial version by contacting the manufacturer, StepWare, at www.acereader.com. You can also look at a program called e-Read from www.kerus.com. It is similar to AceReader.

Many people are afraid to speed-read technical material. Day 9 focuses on how to build background knowledge and vocabulary so technical material is easier to read and comprehend.

Reading on a
Technical Track

Race cars either race on oval tracks or road courses. The oval tracks are easier to race on because the track width accommodates many cars, the distance from corner to corner is predictable, and the driver can safely know when to speed up or slow down.

Road courses are more challenging to race on because they are not one specific shape, there is not as much room, only one car can go around a corner at a time, and there are more, unpredictable, and sharper corners. A driver then needs to be even more patient and aware of what is going on in the race and to frequently press the brake pedal. Rookies understandably take a longer time learning how to race on a road course than on an oval track due to a lack of experience and fast driving expertise.

Relating this analogy to reading material, an oval course is that material which is predictable and familiar. More technical material, which has little or no predictability and is unfamiliar, may be compared to a road course.

What's "Technical"?

What is meant by "technical" reading material? It depends on the reader. Though I am an efficient reader, sit me down next to a medical researcher reading a technical, detailed pharmaceutical study and the researcher will read faster and comprehend the material much better than I. This is because the researcher's background knowledge in that area, including familiarity with the structure of these studies and their vocabulary, is much broader than mine.

Think of technical material as material with unfamiliar vocabulary or terminology, numbers or statistics you must know, or completely new information. Examples include a computer manual describing how to operate a new software program, or a report describing the state of the economy, or a feasibility study done on a company's new long-term development plan.

How much of your reading is truly this technical? I venture to guess, depending on your profession and interests, what you have considered technical up until now is not truly technical. Instead, it is information you need to spend time studying, learning, and applying, not just getting an idea. Reading anything with the purpose of building a bridge of knowledge from new information to old takes more time and an intentional use of active reading strategies. Any previous experience or knowledge makes the reading less technical.

Many of my workshop participants tell me they feel uncomfortable reading technical material fast. And rightfully so. When you read truly technical material, you are unfamiliar with its contents and most likely need to learn it for a test, a work-related project, or other important applications. Reading it as quickly as material you are familiar with is unrealistic and, in some cases, unwise.

You can, however, read and understand technical material more efficiently. This means using active reading strategies to get what you need as quickly as you can. In the end you have a greater understanding of the material in a shorter period of time. Though you do have to read technical material more slowly than with material you understand, there are several strategies you can use to help you read faster, expand your background knowledge and vocabulary, and help avoid the need to read the material several times.

 ## Fast Tracks: Getting More Background Knowledge

Individuals who start new jobs, within the same company or in a different organization, sometimes feel as if they are in a foreign land when they read company material. Because they lack background knowledge of the organization's policies, procedures, acronyms, and vocabulary, reading technical material is a challenge on average for the first six months. After that time, the employee gains experience, resulting in background knowledge to make reading more efficient and comfortable.

If technical material is considered technical because of a lack of familiarity, then it would make sense to find ways to build background knowledge to make your reading more efficient. Many of the following suggestions will already be familiar to you.

- **Pre-view!** Once again, pre-viewing (Day 5) to the rescue. Even the most unfamiliar text is less threatening after pre-viewing. Pre-viewing is a great way to get familiar with the layout of the text, an overview of the contents, and the author's progression of ideas before you jump in reading from detail to detail.

- **Become familiar with unfamiliar terms.** Pre-viewing helps you identify any words or acronyms that are unfamiliar to you. If you are reading a textbook, you often find vocabulary words printed in bold, in a margin, or in a list at the beginning or end of a chapter. In business reading, trust that any unfamiliar words will jump out at you when you skim your eyes down through the paragraphs. By taking the time to find out and even write down the meaning of these terms *before* you read in detail, you have begun to understand the reading's contents and the process of learning these words.

- **Identify your purpose and responsibility.** Depending on your purpose and responsibility, you may not need to understand, learn, or remember everything you read. The only way to know is to continuously remember why you are reading the material and what you need it for.

- **Look for 5W's and H.** Instead of reading from the beginning to end hoping some meaning jumps out at you, take this proactive approach by looking for the answers to the 5W's and H—who, what, when, where, why, and how. Many times, finding the answers to only these questions is sufficient. Also, they help you quickly identify unfamiliar vocabulary terms, pertinent examples, and related ideas.

- **Modify a faster reading strategy.** Just because the material is technical doesn't mean you should abandon all faster reading strategies and go back to reading word for word. You can still use key words, phrases, key phrases, or a pacer, but at a slower speed. All of these strategies are extremely useful as a means to identify the more important words or phrases, which build comprehension, and to help keep your place in the thick jungle of unfamiliar ideas.

- **Re-view.** You create long-term memory recall through repetition over time. If your goal is to make the material a part of your long-term memory, your permanent background knowledge, you have to expose yourself to the information many times. Re-viewing is best done a short time after you have pre-viewed and read in detail. Re-viewing follows the same process as pre-viewing except the purpose is not to introduce you to the material but rather to review or solidify what you know. At the same time, you identify information you still don't know. Constant exposure to the material is similar to re-viewing. To practice, try:

- Talking about the material.
- Reading other material related to it.
- Applying the information.
- Sharing it with someone.
- Listening to a tape about it.
- Watching a video or news broadcast about it.
- Taking a class on it.

If you crammed for school exams, leaving all your studying till the night before, you may have grasped enough to get by on the test but probably forgot most of the material the next week. If you had to use it again in another class or added more information to what you already were exposed to, then you had a better chance of remembering it longer.

The More Words the Better

What do you do when you come across a word you don't know? You might immediately go to a dictionary or just skip it. Others use the "walking dictionary" approach of asking someone else if they know what a word means. Some try to figure it out in context, by using contextual clues. Others try to sound the word out to see if it rings a bell to them that way. A select few use the clues provided in parts of words such as prefixes, suffixes, and roots to identify its meaning.

The more words you know, the easier it is to read faster with good comprehension. When workshop participants or clients ask me what the youngest age I work with is, I say seventh grade. Prior to seventh grade, students don't have enough known vocabulary words built up in their background knowledge to make reading faster possible. Also, if a person consistently has a comprehension average lower than 70 percent, determined by using a ten-question format similar to the one found in this book, then a lack of vocabulary is suspected.

I frequently have participants in my programs for whom English is their second language. Their ability to increase their reading speed with the same or better comprehension is completely dependent upon the breadth of their English vocabulary. Also, these participants are happily relieved when they learn how to read key words or thoughts instead of processing English one tedious word at a time.

Learning anything new takes time, including new words. It is easier when you depend on what you already know as a basis for building more vocabulary. Remember brain glue from Day 2. Let's take a look at the pros and cons of each strategy.

Skipping Words

Skipping unfamiliar words is sometimes a valuable use of your time. If the word is seemingly unimportant to what you are reading or you get the idea without knowing what a word means, then finding its meaning wastes your time. If, however, you are actively trying to build your vocabulary, then it is a good idea to write the word and its definition down in a special place just for tracking new words.

Using a Dictionary

Using a dictionary is a great way to learn new vocabulary *if* you remember the word and its meaning after just one exposure. I believe the best use of a dictionary is as a confirmation tool to check if what you think the word means is correct. And when all else fails, meaning no other self-directed method works, then of course use the dictionary.

To make the mechanical process of looking up words in the dictionary more mindful, write the term down with its definition in a separate notebook and review it from time to time. Intentionally find opportunities to use the word(s) in conversations. Repetitive exposure to the terms over time will imprint them in your background knowledge.

Instead of going to a dictionary, try relying on your brain first. If you can figure the meaning of a word on your own the first time, you can figure it out again without a dictionary.

All words are made up of prefixes, roots, and suffixes. By learning these parts of words, you will be more capable of figuring out word meanings without a dictionary.

Here are some common prefixes, roots, and suffixes. Each is shown with its meaning and an example. If you do not know what the example means, then you might want to look it up in the dictionary. Note that roots can also start a word because not all words have a prefix.

Prefixes	Meaning	Examples
anti	against	antithesis, antibody
pre	before	premonition, predispose

Roots	Meaning	Examples
aud	hear	audible, auditorium
omni	all	omniscient, omnipotent

Suffixes	Meaning	Examples
able, ible	capable of	portable, adaptable
ation	the act of	exasperation, coordination

There are many books and audiotape programs available for building your vocabulary. Look in your local bookstore or library for possibilities. For example, you might try *10 Days to a More Powerful Vocabulary*, which is part of the same series as this book.

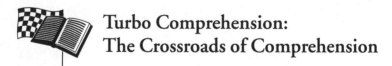 ## Turbo Comprehension: The Crossroads of Comprehension

Having to understand technical material is challenging. Don't let anyone tell you otherwise. It's just like studying for a test when the purpose is to not only understand but also to apply the information. Up until now, you may not have felt confident or competent with technical material because you had little previous experience with the information.

Remember that your comprehension of any material, including technical, improves when you are able to:

• Select and understand what you need for your purpose and responsibility.

- Retain and recall the appropriate information depending on your purpose and responsibility.
- Connect new information to existing knowledge.

Understanding material doesn't mean passively memorizing information because you might need it someday. Remember that memorizing only puts the information into short-term memory anyway. It doesn't mean you need to read every word. It means you have to put the active reading strategies into play more than ever.

Types of Comprehension

When you say you understood what you read, it means you understood in one of three ways:

1. Literally
2. Interpretively
3. Applied

Take the statement "I'm so hungry I could eat a horse." If you understood this literally, you would think I was so hungry that I was going to eat a real horse. If you interpreted what was said, you would understand that I was just *really* hungry. And if you applied the meaning, you might ask me if I'd like something to eat.

Young children generally have only a literal level of understanding. As they grow older and expand their experiences, they come to understand the interpretive and applied levels on their own.

Another example of these levels relates to a student's learning. When learning a foreign language (or any other discipline), you start with the basics—vocabulary and verb conjunctions. You literally memorize the word and its meaning and respond accordingly on a matching or multiple choice test. Once you learn the foundational words, you move into sentences and paragraphs and see how the words fit together to form meaning. You are asked to interpret more of the language and take tests with fill-in-the-blank questions or that require short answers. And finally, when you have a stronger command of the language, you are then asked to *apply* what you know in conversation or on longer essays or papers.

You can apply technical material when you ask yourself questions such as, "So what does this really mean?" or "How does this affect XYZ?" or "In what way can I use this?" Take your knowledge to its highest level by seeking out possible ways to apply or use the information.

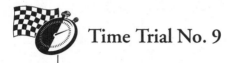 ## Time Trial No. 9

Once again, it's time to test your engine. It should take you five minutes or less. Remember to add pre-viewing into the process.

On the following practice reading, experiment with some of the information you have learned. Try using key words, phrases, key phrases, or a pacer. Ensure an appropriate environment for uninterrupted successful reading.

1. **Pre-view the reading first.** Time yourself for a maximum of only thirty seconds, allowing yourself to quickly look at the introduction, the first sentences of the paragraphs, and the questions you will be answering.

2. **Time yourself.** See how long it takes to read the passage "A Few Words" below. Write your total time in minutes

and seconds in the space provided at the end of the reading.

A Few Words

By John D. Whitman

There are two kinds of words that everyone can identify: old-fashioned words that can become obscure in modern times or change and modern words that mean something to everyone. We all understand, for example, what a "dollar" is, but if you talk about "ducats," a type of money used several centuries ago, only historians are likely to understand.

But there's a third type of word: old-fashioned words whose original meanings have been replaced by more modern definitions. For example, imagine driving to your local gym to work out so you'll develop washboard abs. On the way you hit a pothole in the road. You can probably define the words "gym," "washboard," and "pothole." But your definitions are likely to be very different from the original definitions of these words—all of which are as outdated as the manual typewriter.

You might be surprised, for instance, to know that the original tradition of working out at a gym meant you'd have to do it in the nude, because a *gymnast* literally means a "naked person." The ancient Greeks preferred it that way. Very few of us can really get washboard abs and even fewer have used an actual *washboard*—the ribbed board used to scrub clothes in the days before washing machines.

Potholes originally referred to holes in the tops of old-fashioned stoves. When you wanted to cook something, you moved the lid and placed a pot over the pothole so that the fire could reach it directly.

Here are a few more words that may seem current to you, but have actually evolved from years ago. Try dialing a phone. In this digital age, most phones are push-button, but we still use the word "dial," which refers to the round disk with finger holes on the front of old-fashioned telephones. Even the experts call most Internet-access points "dial-up servers," even though no one's dialing anything anymore.

How about storage for computers. If you hide your computer in that popular piece of home furniture called the office armoire, you're storing your laptop where your ancestors stored the sword. "Armoire" is the French word for armory.

We're bound to hold on to outdated words because their meanings are familiar and comfortable. We simply apply them in a new context. So, as you hurtle down the computer superhighway, just remember to still watch for potholes.

Mark your reading time here: _____ (minutes) _____ (seconds).

3. **Respond to statements.** Immediately answer the following statements to the best of your ability WITHOUT looking back at the reading. Estimate the number of answers you believe are correct and put the number in the blank provided.

Comprehension Statements

Without looking back at the reading passage, respond to the following statements by indicating whether the statement is True (T), False (F), or Not Discussed (N).

_____ 1. There are two types of words everyone can identify: old-fashioned words and words that mean something to everyone.

_____ 2. The word "ducat" is a new term.

_____ 3. In ancient Greece, it was forbidden to work out in a gym in the nude.

_____ 4. There are potholes on most major roadways.

_____ 5. Washboards are used in gyms to clean soiled towels.

_____ 6. Placing a pot over a hole in an old-fashioned stove would put the fire out.

_____ 7. We keep the term "dial" in our vocabulary because some people still use telephones with the round dials on the front.

_____ 8. The term "armoire" is derived from the French word for armory.

_____ 9. It is likely that we will continue to develop new meanings for old terms.

_____ 10. We hold on to outdated words because we don't want to go to the effort of creating new terms.

Now, estimate how many of these answers you believe you have correct out of ten _____.

4. **Check your responses.** Turn to the Answer Key on page 202. If you have any incorrect, mark the correct response and return to the reading passage to try to understand where you had a problem.

5. **Figure your comprehension percent.** Add the total number of correct responses you have and multiply by 10. Write your comprehension percentage in your Personal Progress chart on page 206.

6. **Figure your Words per Minute.** Look at your reading time and round off the seconds to the nearest 10-second mark. Turn to the Words per Minute chart on page 207 and find your Words per Minute next to your reading time. Write your Words per Minute in your Personal Progress chart.

7. **Track your Time Trial scores.** Go to your Personal Progress chart and make sure you've recorded your Words per Minute, comprehension percentage, and the date you did the exercise. It's also helpful to document other details such as time of day, any preoccupations, strategies used, and so on.

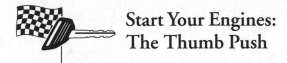

Start Your Engines:
The Thumb Push

There are two ways to perform the pacer known as the Thumb Push. Choose a page in a magazine, newspaper, or this book to experiment with. Make sure to place it on a flat surface, not balanced upright in your hands.

The first method is "thumb down," the other is "thumb across." Begin thumb down by positioning your hand: Make a loose, relaxed fist in front of you with whichever hand you want to read with. Stick your thumb out to the side. Now rotate your thumb toward you so your thumb is pointing downward, creating a thumb-down sign. Place your hand with the thumb down above the column you are going to read. Your thumb should be pointed down in the center of the column. Begin reading, stopping your eyes only two or three times on each line, seeing more at a glance. Remember to use key words, phrases, or key phrases to help you go even faster. As you become more accustomed to the method, try moving your thumb a little faster.

The thumb across method starts the same as thumb down by creating a fist with your chosen hand and sticking your thumb out to the side. This time leave the thumb in this position and place it above the line you are going to start reading. You should have somewhat of a straight line from your wrist to the tip of your thumb, covering the words you already read and leaving open where you are going. This is very similar to the white card method. Therefore, if you want to use the white card method and there is no card around, use your own wrist and thumb.

Gauge Your Attitude

Let's take an attitude check. Write down or mentally fill in the blank of the following statement:

> I am a(n) _____ reader.

Is your reading attitude changing?

 ## Pit Stop: Tip of the Day

Look for different ways to experience the world. The more you experience, the more background knowledge you have. And this in turn helps you read faster with better comprehension. You could plan vacations to places you have never been, read books on topics you normally do not have interest in, expose yourself to educational television programs you may not normally watch, speak to lots of people and tap into their background knowledge, learn a new skill, take a class, and so on. Your ability to expand your background knowledge is only limited by your willingness to explore new horizons.

In Day 10, you will evaluate your progress looking at your reading speed and habits. In addition, you will receive one final tip to carry you into the world of reading.

The Final Lap

Here you are, the white flag is being waved, just one more lap until the race is over. At this point, you are on the final sprint to the finish line. As you complete the race, give yourself a hearty pat on the back because you finally did something to make faster reading a reality. You read this book, tried new strategies, timed yourself, and gathered information to make your reading workload more manageable. Your racing career, though, is far from over. It is only just beginning.

As a reader and student of this book, you are similar to a race car driver in training. This day completes your formal training, but to become truly skilled, you continually need to experiment with the strategies and learn through trial and error what works for you in your own world. If you listen to motivational speakers such as Tony Robbins or Zig Ziglar or sales gurus such as Tom Hopkins or Brian Tracy, you hear them all tout the value of daily reading. Brian Tracy says if you have an hour's commute each day and listen to instructional or motivational tapes, you can learn a semester's worth of material in six months. I've heard other experts say if you read a half hour every day for two years or an hour a day for a year you become an authority in any subject in which you have interest. They agree that reading is crucial to success in your field. Let's assume they are referring to average untrained readers; I wonder how a faster reading speed coupled with other efficient reading skills affects the outcome.

It is important to remind you that your past is not predictive of your future. If you have always read slowly, it doesn't mean you will read slowly your whole life—unless you choose to. Before you started this book, you didn't have much choice. Now you do. You now know what makes faster reading a reality—if you choose. By following the strategies in this book and adapting them to your world, you can become a faster and more efficient reader.

Reading for Survival

One thing is certain and more so these days than ever: Change is constant and technological innovations are at the forefront of this progress. Developing technologies, especially the World Wide Web, are transforming the economy, forcing you, the worker, to continually rationalize, reinvent, and restructure your work. How can you get help to cope with this change? Through reading.

Employers are demanding that you constantly acquire new skills but few provide the training or time required to obtain these skills. The unemployable of the (near) future will be those who can't, or don't learn, regardless of available learning resources. Where can you learn these skills? Through reading.

You must realize and accept the reality that technology will affect you even though you wish it wouldn't. Being proactive with respect to this change is much better than being reactive. How can you become proactive and adapt to changing technologies? Through reading.

The ability to communicate and work effectively with others is also a workplace necessity with the advent of work teams. How can you learn to manage diverse personalities and other interpersonal issues? Through reading.

The information found through reading provides you with options to help you solve problems, cope with change, learn new skills, and most importantly, better understand the world you live in.

Reading, unlike taking a class, is done according to your own schedule. You choose what you need to read and decide which parts to skip or spend your time on. The material is there to refer back to, if needed, and no one tests you on what they think you should know. You decide. The world is literally at your fingertips when you choose to read.

The "Other" Reading Material

You already know about your reading pile. But there is "other" material you read that you probably don't consider reading, either because it doesn't make it to the pile or you just process it as it arrives such as regular mail or e-mail. These present you with more opportunities to play with your new reading techniques and use some of the tips discussed in this book. Here's a sampling of other materials you may read:

At Home

- Homeowner manuals
- Credit card applications
- Appliance warranties
- Membership applications
- Tax forms
- School applications

- Directions for toys or furniture assembly
- Insurance policies
- Financial documents

At Work

- Proposals
- Patient charts
- Legal documents
- Corporate profiles
- Reports
- Insurance policies
- Business plans
- Résumés
- Complaint letters
- Interoffice memos
- Internet research

At School

- Textbooks
- Literature
- Reading comprehension tests
- Library and Internet research
- Reference material

If you've ever been admitted to a hospital, you may recall the lengthy and vital forms you were asked to sign. The hospital employee processing the paperwork tells you what it says and points to the dotted line. Most people sign the forms without reading. With your faster reading skills, you can now read these and other legal documents quickly, making sure you agree with what you are signing.

Where Are You Now?

It's been ten days since you started your reading training. The following section will help you gauge where you are right now.

1. **Facts and figures.** In Day 1, you evaluated yourself statistically in your Words per Minute and comprehension on the first Time Trial. Your Personal Progress chart on page 203 shows your development with your reading scores. Now, it is time to do the last Time Trial to see where you are. Turn to and do Time Trial No. 10 on page 192.

  - What seems to be working?
  - What strategies are you comfortable with?
  - What do you want to become more comfortable with?

2. **Efficiency.** In Day 2, you had the opportunity to evaluate yourself on the "Inefficient and Efficient Reader checklist." Go back to that list now (page 19) and use a different color pen to redo the checklist according to how you feel today. Do you have more checks on the efficient side? If so, what are you doing to achieve this? If not, what is preventing you? Remember that learning to be more efficient is a process, not a one-time event. Any progress on your process is a step in the right direction.

3. **Attitude.** Starting in Day 1 and every day throughout this book, you were asked to gauge your attitude. Now is the last time to reevaluate your attitude:

"I am a(n) _____ reader."

Are your words more positive, competent, and confident than when you began? If so, what is making you feel or think this way? If not, what is preventing you from feeling or thinking this way? If you only read a few chapters or didn't do any of the exercises, take the time to go back and do them. Insecurity about your newfound potential is common; certainty comes with experience.

What Are Your Keepers?

Whenever you go to a conference, listen to an audiotape training, read a nonfiction book, or experience any other learning forum, always be on the lookout for solid ideas or actions that you can take away from the experience. Otherwise, you are wasting your time. When I attend conferences, training, or professional meetings, I not only make a list of things to take away but I sometimes create a list of keepers or to-do's. What are you going to take away or do as a result of reading this book?

The following is a list of possible reading commitments you can make as a result of your experience with this book. They are broken down into three areas: reading awareness, reading and time management, and reading strategies. It takes ten minutes or less to complete this exercise.

1. Review each list that follows in its entirety.

2. Identify and check the items you want to commit yourself to. You can also write them on a separate piece of paper. Feel free to adapt them or add your own.

3. Schedule a date next month and then for the following three months or more to quickly review and revise your reading commitment. Use this menu as a guide in your revision.

Reading Awareness

☐ 1. I will accept that I'm human and capable of a few natural mistakes.

☐ 2. I will be aware of my eye movements involved in the reading process.

☐ 3. I want my eyes to stop on the more important words in the text.

☐ 4. I want to remember the relationship between background knowledge and reading comprehension.

☐ 5. I will read in a quiet, distraction-free environment.

☐ 6. I will read without listening to music (unless it's Mozart or other classical music).

☐ 7. I will always know my purpose and responsibility before I begin to read.

☐ 8. I will not read for work or school with the television on.

☐ 9. I will read work or study materials at a desk or table.

☐ 10. I will read leisure material anywhere and anytime I want.

☐   11. I will reevaluate my lighting and make it friendly for my eyes.

☐   12. I will get my eyes checked every two years by an optometrist.

☐   13. I will be aware of and take care of my mental and physical distractions before I read.

☐   14. I will try to relax when I have a lot of reading to do.

☐   15. I will remember the difference between skimming and scanning.

☐   16. I will be able to skip information without guilt.

☐   17. I will be aware of my reading speed and shift it depending on my purpose and background knowledge.

☐   18. I will reevaluate what I consider truly technical material.

☐   19. I will enjoy reading more.

☐   20. I will: _____.

Reading and Time Management

☐   1. I will find time to read.

☐   2. I will resist the temptation to pick up the phone while reading.

☐   3. I will resist the temptation to check on incoming faxes.

☐   4. I will resist the temptation to check e-mail the moment it notifies me of incoming messages.

☐   5. I will always carry reading material with me.

☐   6. I will listen to audiotapes for personal or professional development.

☐   7. I will avoid marathon reading sessions by taking short, frequent breaks.

☐   8. If I come across usable information, I will immediately make note of it either on the material or in a notebook.

☐   9. I will create a reference system for keeping track of important usable reading material.

☐   10. I will: _____.

Reading Strategies

Note: You may have more than one answer for some of the questions.

1. I will reduce passive daydreaming when I read by

☐   a. Reading faster

☐   b. Reading key words, phrases, and key phrases

☐   c. Using a pacer

2. I will reduce going back over material (regression) I already read by

☐   a. Reading faster

☐   b. Reading key words, phrases, and key phrases

☐   c. Using a pacer

3. I will reduce the talking in my head (mental whispering/subvocalization) by

☐   a. Reading faster

☐   b. Reading key words, phrases, and key phrases

☐   c. Using a pacer

☐   4. I will stop moving my lips by placing my finger to my lips while I read.

☐   5. I will personally choose only quality material for my reading pile.

☐   6. I will reduce my to read stack by

☐   a. Using the "One Month Tracker"

☐   b. Pre-viewing everything

☐   c. Getting myself removed from invaluable mailing lists

☐   d. Canceling subscriptions

☐   e. Throwing away junk mail right away

☐   f. Copying or cutting out interesting articles

☐   g. Limiting the number of books I buy

☐   h. Using efficient reading techniques

☐   i. I will: _____.

☐   7. I will use a pacer to help me read faster.

☐   8. I will resist the temptation to print off the computer screen.

☐   9. I will read more on the computer screen.

☐   10. I will use the note-making tools only when I think I might need to refer back to the information again.

☐   11. I will continue to question the author's point of view.

☐   12. I will be aware of my opinions, inferences, and biases.

☐   13. I want to become an active, mindful, and conscious reader.

☐   14. I will: _____.

Time Trial No. 10

For the final lap, let's evaluate your engine. It should take you five minutes or less. On the following practice reading, experiment with some of the information you have learned about. Try using key words, phrases, key phrases, or a pacer. Ensure an appropriate environment for uninterrupted successful reading.

1. **Pre-view the reading first.** Time yourself for a maximum of only thirty seconds, allowing yourself to quickly look at the introduction, the first sentences of the paragraphs, and the questions you will be answering.

2. **Time yourself.** See how long it takes to read the passage "April Fool's Day: A Real Kick in the Pants!" below. Write your total time in minutes and seconds in the space provided at the end of the reading.

April Fool's Day: A Real Kick in the Pants!

By John D. Whitman

Mark Twain once wrote, "The first of April is the day we remember what we are the other 364 days of the year." That day is, of course, April Fool's Day. On that day, schoolchildren might tell a classmate that school has been canceled, or point down and say, "Your shoe's untied!" More elaborate jokes involve sending the victim on a "fool's errand" to find something that doesn't exist. A modern variation of the fool's errand is "snark hunting," where a group in the know sends a hapless individual out into the woods looking for a nonexistent animal.

Where did April Fool's Day originate? Centuries ago, many people in European cultures celebrated the New Year at the beginning of spring. This celebration usually took place in March near the spring equinox. Since spring is a time of renewal, this new year celebration made sense.

When Pope Gregory introduced the modern calendar in 1562, moving New Year's Day to January 1, most Europeans readily adopted the new calendar. However, those who refused to use it and, even better, those who forgot about the switch, were labeled fools. They were sent fake party invitations and given prank gifts on the old New Year's Day.

The tradition of pulling pranks on April 1 survived long after the memory of the original meaning was forgotten. In France, April 1 is called "Poisson d'avril." French schoolchildren try to fool their comrades by taping a paper fish to their backs. When the classmate discovers the trick, all his friends cry out "Poisson d'avril!," which means "April Fish!"

The idea of April Fool's Day is celebrated in Mexico as well, but for different reasons and even on a different day. In Mexico, December 28 is "El Día de los Inocentes." It is set aside as a day for Christians to mourn Herod's slaughter of innocent children. Over the years, the tone of that solemn day changed from sadness to good-natured trickery.

In Scotland, April Fool's Day actually lasts two days. The second day is dedicated to pranks. Some aspects of this second fool's day survive in our most cherished traditional practical jokes. If you've ever had anyone tape a "Kick Me" sign to your back on April Fool's Day, you can thank the Scots for every boot on your bottom.

Today's best pranks don't hurt anyone, and delivered in the right spirit, they usually leave even the victim laughing.

Mark your reading time here: _____ (minutes) _____ (seconds).

3. **Respond to statements.** Immediately answer the following statements to the best of your ability WITHOUT looking back at the reading. Estimate the number of answers you believe are correct and put the number in the blank provided.

Comprehension Statements

Without looking back at the reading passage, respond to the following statements by indicating whether the statement is True (T), False (F), or Not Discussed (N).

_____ 1. When New Year's Day was moved on the calendar to January 1, those who continued to celebrate it on April 1 were considered fools.

_____ 2. On the ancient calendar, April Fool's Day signaled the beginning of the new year.

_____ 3. Today, children participate in April Fool's Day coloring contests.

_____ 4. Before the modern calendar was introduced, people were imprisoned if they didn't celebrate New Year's Day on January 1.

_____ 5. In France, April Fool's translates into April Fish.

_____ 6. Mexico celebrates April Fool's Day on March 28, just before the traditional April 1.

_____ 7. Sweden celebrates two April Fool's Days.

_____ 8. Scotland is responsible for the "Kick Me" sign prank.

_____ 9. Studies indicate that April Fool's pranks will become less innocent in future years.

_____ 10. April Fool's Day began in the 1500s.

Now, estimate how many of these answers you believe you have correct out of ten _____.

4. **Check your responses.** Turn to the Answer Key on page 202. If you have any incorrect, mark the correct response and return to the reading passage to try to understand where you had a problem.

5. **Figure your comprehension percentage.** Add the total number of correct responses you have and multiply by 10. Write your comprehension percentage in your Personal Progress chart on page 206.

6. **Figure your Words per Minute.** Look at your reading time and round off the seconds to the nearest 10-second mark. Turn to the Words per Minute chart on page 207 and find your Words per Minute next to your reading time. Write your Words per Minute in your Personal Progress chart.

7. **Track your Time Trial scores.** Go to your Personal Progress chart and make sure you've recorded your Words per Minute, comprehension percentage, and the date you did the exercise. It's also helpful to document other details such as time of day, any preoccupations, strategies used, and so on.

 ## Fast Tracks: How to Figure Reading Speed on Your Own

After completing the readings in this book, check on your progress from time to time. I have several suggestions.

- **To gauge both reading speed and comprehension.** Purchase a timed reading workbook, such as from Jamestown Publishers at 1-800-USA-Read. Any book in the Timed Reading Plus series is closest in length and content to the readings in this book.

- **To check your reading speed.** Use your own reading material. Use material where the column width is consistent, such as a newspaper column.

1. **Figure your average words per line:** Choose any 10 lines of text and count the number of words in each line and divide by 10. If your total is 79 words, then the average words per line is 7.9 words, or round higher to 8 words per line. If your total is 93 words, then the average words per line is 9.3, or round lower to 9 words per line.

2. **Time yourself.** Read for exactly one minute.

3. **Figure your words per minute.** Count the number of lines you have read and multiply them by the average number of words per line. Number of lines read times average words per line equals words per minute.

- To figure how long it will take you to read a novel, follow these steps:

  1. **Time yourself.** Read a book for ten minutes. Count the number of pages you read.

  2. **Figure your average time per page.** Take the 10 minutes and divide it by the number of pages you read. If you read 8 pages, then divide 10 by 8. 10 divided by 8 is 1.25 or 1 minute 15 seconds. The average time per page is 1 minute 15 seconds.

  3. **Figure your total time.** Multiply the number of pages in the book by 1.25. If the book has 230 pages, then 230 pages × 1.25 per page = 287.5 total minutes. If you want to know hours and minutes, then divide the total minutes by 60. 287.5 ÷ 60 = 4.79. This ends up being 4.79 hours or approximately 4 hours and 45 minutes.

The Last Words About Leisure Reading Material

Leisure reading material is whatever you choose to read, not what work or school dictates. Though many people read non-fiction for leisure, many more people choose to read fiction. Here are a few tips or reminders to keep in mind when reading fiction:

1. Don't skim or pre-view.

2. Choose your own reading speed.

3. Read anywhere you want.

4. Fast-forward through the boring parts.

5. Read dialogue or poetry slower or even word for word to get the true essence of what is being said or how it is being expressed.

 ## Turbo Comprehension: INCORP Model

If you work within a group or a team of people who have a similar career, chances are you read or need to read the same material. The INCORP model helps you and your team stay current in your field, eliminate reading redundancy, spark creative synergy and communication, and encourage teamwork. Use this model and adapt it to suit your group's working style. INCORP is an acronym:

- Identify what you should be reading.
- Network with others in your field. Find out what others read, what organizations they belong to, and what publications they receive. List them all. Then decide

which are the best use of your time and the most valuable to your profession.

- Collect the material, which may result in ordering new subscriptions or canceling multiples or invaluable ones.

- Organize a reading team. Divide the material by deciding among yourselves who reads what. If someone prefers to read the business newspaper but dislikes professional journals, then let him read the newspaper. Rotate reading assignments for variety.

- Read the material in a timely manner looking for business-related information. It is also helpful to know a little about the personal interests of each team member so you can read with them in mind. If you know a team member is designing a beach house and you come across information about a new building material, you can share it with him.

- Process the information. Decide to meet weekly, biweekly, or monthly to discuss your findings. You may decide to just photocopy the articles and circulate them among the others in your group. If everyone knows how to pre-view, the article will get passed around faster. If you are doing research reading, type up your findings by listing the article, source, date, and a brief summary of the information presented.

If you put this model into practice, you stay current while reducing an individual's reading workload.

Some companies form reading groups. For example, a popular business book is distributed to each member of a work team. Every week, they meet for an hour, usually Friday, to read and discuss how the book affects their business. What a great way to participate in your own career and the direction your company takes.

Start Your Engines:
The Two Finger Sway

The Two Finger Sway is the most advanced pacer presented in this book. It assumes that you know how to see more at a glance and are comfortable incorporating two or three lines of text at a time.

Choose something to read. Make the peace sign with your index finger and middle finger of either hand and then put the two fingers together. Tuck your other three fingers into your palm. Place the two fingers under the first line of the paragraph and move your fingers across the line with your eyes. When you get to the end of the line, drop your fingers down several lines of text and begin reading where your fingers are. Try reading more than just the line you are on. It *is* possible. Move your fingers with your eyes across that line and again move them down several lines. Your hand zigzags or sways as your reading flows. Go faster as you get more comfortable. Use this method for doing a fast skim or pre-view. Avoid moving your fingers across every line to stop yourself from reading, which slows you down.

Pit Stop: Tip of the Day

At the end of my programs, I tell a true story about when and how I decided to get into the faster reading profession. I include it here because it shares a powerful message.

It was Christmas 1988 and I had no real career direction. I was making a living by working temp jobs, substitute teaching, and waitressing. I was going through outplacement counseling to identify my strengths and which careers matched my abilities. During this time, I was thinking about starting a training business to help busy people manage their reading workload but I wasn't sure if it would succeed. A career in teaching faster reading didn't show up on my job list probably because it's not a typical job. Did people really need to read faster as I had believed? And could I help them?

Being the holidays, I was feeling depressed, with little money to spend and no clear career direction. I was eating Chinese takeout with my boyfriend—now my husband, Christopher—and discussing my situation. He said something I'll never forget: "The universe has a plan for you. Just look for the signs. A sign," he said, "could be as obvious as something someone says, or as hidden as a coincidence that might not be a coincidence at all." I looked at him with a somewhat confused look, shrugged my shoulders, and said, "Okay."

At the end of our meal, he held out his hand with four fortune cookies in it. I picked one, secretly hoping, as I always do, that what it says will bring me luck. I opened the cookie and read the fortune. My jaw dropped, and my eyes widened. I said, "I think I found the sign I was looking for to decide whether or not I should go into this business." The fortune said:

The road to knowledge begins with the turn of a page.

And so, as a result of reading this book, I hope you are able to turn more pages, which will put you solidly on the road to knowledge.

Answer Key

Day 1: All About Reading

    1. F, 2. T, 3. T, 4. T, 5. F, 6. N, 7. N, 8. F, 9. T, 10. T

Day 2: Battling the Worry Bug

    1. F, 2. T, 3. T, 4. N, 5. F, 6. T, 7. T, 8. N, 9. N, 10. T

Day 3: A True Athlete

    1. T, 2. F, 3. N, 4. F, 5. F, 6. N, 7. F, 8. N, 9. N, 10. T

Day 4: The History of Speed Reading

    No comprehension questions.

Day 5: Pre-view Day 6

    1. T, 2. F, 3. F, 4. T, 5. N, 6. F, 7. N, 8. T, 9. F, 10. N

Day 6: It's All Relative

    1. F, 2. T, 3. F, 4. T, 5. F, 6. N, 7. T, 8. F, 9. N, 10. F

Day 7: The Ties That Bind

    1. N, 2. T, 3. F, 4. F, 5. T, 6. F, 7. T, 8. F, 9. N, 10. T

Day 8: Scanning

    1. Claude H, 2. Philip J, 3. 3, 4. 868-6800, 5. R E, 6. K R, 7. 531-6233, 8. 6 Thistle La, 9. John I, 10. Sydney M

Day 8: Books Join the Electronic Wave

   1. F, 2. T, 3. F, 4. N, 5. T, 6, F, 7. T, 8. N, 9. F, 10. T

Day 9: A Few Words

   1. T, 2. F, 3. F, 4. N, 5. N, 6. F, 7. F, 8. T, 9. T, 10. F

Day 10: April Fool's Day: A Real Kick in the Pants!

   1. T, 2. F, 3. N, 4. F, 5. T, 6. F, 7. N, 8. T, 9. N, 10. T

Personal Progress

Date	Reading	WPM
_____		_____

Comprehension _____ **%**   **Other details**

(e.g. time of day, strategies used, preoccupation, and so on.)

Example:

Date	Reading	WPM
1/14	Day 3: A True Athlete	265

Comprehension __80__ **%**   **Other details**

I read this at 10:15 A.M. I closed my door, turned on my voice mail, and sat upright at my desk. I had an appointment at 10:30 A.M.

Date	Reading	WPM
_____	Day 1: All About Reading	_____

Comprehension _____ **%**   **Other details**

Date	Reading	WPM
_____	Day 2: Battling the <u>Worry Bug</u>	_____

Comprehension _____ %

Other details

_____

_____

_____

_____

Date	Reading	WPM
_____	Day 3: <u>A True Athlete</u>	_____

Comprehension _____ %

Other details

_____

_____

_____

_____

Date	Reading	WPM
_____	Day 4: The History of <u>Speed Reading</u>	_____

Comprehension _____ %

Other details

_____

_____

_____

_____

Date   **Reading**   **WPM**

_____   Day 5:   _____
                      <u>Pre-view of Day 6</u>

Comprehension _____%   **Other details**

                                        _____

                                        _____

                                        _____

                                        _____

Date   **Reading**   **WPM**

_____   Day 6:   _____
                      <u>It's All Relative</u>

Comprehension _____%   **Other details**

                                        _____

                                        _____

                                        _____

                                        _____

Date   **Reading**   **WPM**

_____   Day 7:   _____
                      <u>The Ties That Bind</u>

Comprehension _____%   **Other details**

                                        _____

                                        _____

                                        _____

                                        _____

Date   **Reading**   **WPM**

_____   Day 8:   _____
                            Books Join the
                            Electronic Wave

Comprehension _____%   **Other details**

                                                       _____

                                                       _____

                                                       _____

                                                       _____

Date   **Reading**   **WPM**

_____   Day 9:   _____
                            A Few Words

Comprehension _____%   **Other details**

                                                       _____

                                                       _____

                                                       _____

                                                       _____

Date   **Reading**   **WPM**

_____   Day 10:   _____
                            April Fool's Day:
                            A Real Kick in
                            the Pants!

Comprehension _____%   **Other details**

                                                       _____

                                                       _____

                                                       _____

                                                       _____

Words per Minute

All timed readings contain approximately 400 words except for Day 4, The History of Speed Reading, and Day 5, Preview Day 6.

Time	WPM	Time	WPM	Time	WPM
.10	2,400	1:30	265	2:50	140
.20	1,200	1:40	240	3:00	135
.30	800	1:50	220	3:10	125
.40	600	2:00	200	3:20	120
.50	480	2:10	185	3:30	115
1:00	400	2:20	170	3:40	110
1:10	345	2:30	160	3:50	105
1:20	300	2:40	150	4:00	100

Below is the Word per Minute chart to use when you preview Day 6. Day 6 has 4,877 words, and time in bold is the instructed preview time for this exercise.

Pre-View Time	WPM	Pre-View Time	WPM	Pre-View Time	WPM
3:00	1625	4:30	1096	6:00	812
3:10	1557	4:40	1055	6:10	792
3:20	1489	4:50	1041	6:20	771
3:30	1421	**5:00**	**975**	6:30	753
3:40	1353	5:10	948	6:40	732
3:50	1285	5:20	921	6:50	711
4:00	1219	5:30	894	7:00	696
4:10	1178	5:40	867		
4:20	1137	5:50	840		

About the Authors

The Philip Lief Group is a book developer based in Princeton, New Jersey, that produces a wide range of language and usage guides, including *Grammar 101, Guide to Pronunciation,* and *Roget's 21st Century Thesaurus.* The Philip Lief Group has been singled out by the *New York Times* for its "consistent bestsellers" and by *Time* magazine for being "bottom-line think tankers."

The Princeton Language Institute is a consortium of experts composed of linguists, lexicographers, writers, teachers, and businesspeople. The institute focuses on developing easy-to-read self-help books in a nonacademic format for writers, businesspeople, and virtually anyone who wants to enhance their communication and language skills. The Princeton Language Institute is based in Princeton, New Jersey.

Corporate productivity specialist **Abby Marks Beale** is the founder of **The Corporate Educator**, a training company that helps busy professionals work smarter, faster, and just plain better (www.TheCorporateEducator.com). She is the creator of **Rev It Up Reading** (www.RevItUpReading.com) a program that gets people up to speed with what they read through workshops, online learning, and self-study products. Abby also authored *Success Skills: Strategies for Study and Lifelong Learning* and is content editor of *Read More Faster. . . . On-Screen.* She resides in Wallingford, Connecticut.